THE SAVVY EXECUTIVE

THE SAVVY EXECUTIVE

THE HANDBOOK COVERING EMPLOYMENT CONTRACTS, COMPENSATION, EXECUTIVE SKILLS, AND MUCH MORE

G. A. FINCH

WINDY CITY PUBLISHERS

THE SAVVY EXECUTIVE
THE HANDBOOK COVERING EMPLOYMENT CONTRACTS, COMPENSATION, EXECUTIVE SKILLS, AND MUCH MORE

Windy City Publishers
2118 Plum Grove Road, #349
Rolling Meadows, IL 60008
www.windycitypublishers.com

Cover Image: © Yauhen 17/Shutterstock

Published in the United States of America

Paperback ISBN:
978-1-941478-76-9

Library of Congress Control Number:
2018964371

iPad is a registered trademark of Apple Inc.
McRib is a registered trademark of McDonald's Corporation

WINDY CITY PUBLISHERS
CHICAGO

CONTENTS

PREFACE

THIS MODEST CONTRIBUTION TO THE business literature on executive and professional development arises from my blogging and my counseling executives and professionals on their employment issues.

As an attorney advising my executive and professional clients on employment agreements and separation agreements, and as a career mentor and coach for a myriad of strivers, young and old, I have found, much to my honor and delight, that such folks have become repeat clients. They contact me for legal, strategic, and professional development advice. Some of their questions and concerns are quite complex and others simply involve applying common sense to thorny situations or understanding the human condition.

After many years of negotiating and drafting employment and separation agreements for either the executives or the companies that were hiring or firing them, and after many years of advising perplexed executives and professionals on how to survive and thrive in their careers, I now believe that I have something to say that will be of some value to readers at any stage of their careers. Readers will learn some technical things about employment contracts, non-compete agreements, confidentiality agreements, and more. They will learn some soft skills like networking and staying physically and mentally fit to maximize their career success. It is all important "stuff" in service of the executive's or professional's security, advancement, and development. Enjoy your read.

PART I

LEGAL CONSIDERATIONS AND NEGOTIATIONS

FIRST THINGS FIRST: THE EMPLOYMENT CONTRACT

Executive Employment Agreements Are Not Automatic

I know of many aborted CEO executive employment agreement efforts. The negotiations were benign or non-existent. The terms were neither onerous nor one-sided. The companies simply pulled the plug and decided not to move forward with the employment contracts. What gives? Is this the start of a trend? Hardly. Because of continued economic uncertainty, an organization's board of directors is likely to be more risk-averse, to feel more non-committal, and to believe that they — the board of directors — have more bargaining power. Of course, a compelling CEO candidate, who does not need the job, can still demand an employment agreement. Some CEO candidates are so sure of their leadership skills and of their value that they confidently fly naked — they go without an employment agreement. Going naked is not recommended. It is called being an "at-will employee," which means an employer can terminate an employee without any reason or notice. We will explore this employment status further a little bit later in this book.

Before you become the super-duper executive or the highly prized professional, you must get a job offer. Your job offer may come with a proffered employment contract. If not, you should ask for one. A hand-shake and a verbal commitment will not serve you well if the terms of your employment are not remembered or not honored.

Never Start a Job Before the Employment Agreement is Signed

Too many times, a situation in which an executive starts a job with an unfinished employment agreement does not turn out well. Not always the case, but often enough. An executive does not want to be in the percentage of employees who get terminated and who are back in the market without a completed, signed employment agreement that contains a severance payment provision. The executive's relying on the employer to do the right thing, in terms of what the employee thinks the deal was, is not a good choice.

Obviously executives have the most negotiating leverage when a company is seeking to hire them. At the start of the relationship, there is goodwill between the employer and prospective employee and there are high, positive expectations on both sides.

An executive may be eager to demonstrate trust and enthusiasm by agreeing to start while an agreement is being finalized. I know of executives who have quit their prior jobs, forsaken substantial benefits, and relocated to distant cities without a signed agreement. Two scenarios usually are the case. One scenario is that the executive and the employer are still hashing out contract terms after the executive has started employment. Another scenario is the executive has started working and has never received a signed agreement — it falls through the cracks, so to speak.

There is an old saying that "Familiarity breeds contempt." The employer's shiny new executive now has blemishes and scratches upon closer inspection. The sense of urgency has dissipated once the employer has gotten its prized employee. It is human nature to value something less after it has been obtained.

Accordingly, an executive must never start a job without a completely finished, signed agreement in hand. Moreover, whatever "final" employment agreement is tendered, the executive's attorney must review it one last time to make sure that the final draft reflects the latest iteration of the negotiated contract terms. All high-level executives and professionals should use an attorney to help negotiate a final employment agreement. Last-minute language insertions or failure to include agreed-upon provisions can and does happen, sometimes carelessly and in good faith on the part of the employer and sometimes by design. An executive's insistence upon having an executed agreement in hand prior to commencing work is prudent and just common sense. To preserve the executive's ability to maintain a congenial relationship with his or her prospective colleagues or bosses, the executive's attorney should take the responsibility for requiring a signed agreement.

An executive does not want to be in the more difficult position of proving up the terms of an incomplete, unsigned, draft contract in a court of law rather than the easier position of proving up a final, signed contract.

What Does "At-Will" Employment Actually Mean?

Sometimes even knowledgeable executives think they understand a term when they really do not, or they have too much pride to ask for an explanation. Because so much is at stake in understanding the executive employment environment, this chapter provides a convenient primer.

As an example, let us take a look at the law in Illinois, which is a fairly typical jurisdiction in its treatment of employment contract provisions. Illinois is an "at-will" state in terms of employment status. "At-will employment" means, as a general rule, that an employer can fire an employee for no reason. There are five exceptions to this general rule:

1. A union contract

2. An individual contract with a termination-for-cause provision

3. An implied contract, *e.g.*, an employee handbook

4. A public policy violation such as being fired for performing jury duty, serving as a military reservist, filing a workers' compensation claim, refusing to carry out an illegal act, or "blowing the whistle"

5. A violation of civil rights laws concerning race, sex, disability, religion, sexual orientation, *etc.*

Thus the at-will employment concept is simultaneously both simple and complicated.

Agreement and Benefits Checklist (Not Exhaustive)

Some executives, professionals, and employers find it useful to have a handy list of provisions and items to consider in an employment agreement or a discussion of benefits. Below are the usual suspects, plus a few that reflect the particular interests expressed by the employee or the particular benefits offered by the employer. The kind of perk or benefit is limited only by the imagination of the executive negotiator. The first nine items are your big and fundamental provisions or benefits that you must have upfront clarity and understanding about in order to ascertain whether a job opportunity makes sense to you as the executive or professional.

Threshold Items

1   Position Title, Duties, and Responsibilities

The title, duties, and responsibilities of the position must be set out clearly, including reporting responsibilities. There have been many employees who thought they had a certain job title, like CEO, only to discover upon commencing work that the company had given them a different, usually insufficient, job title.

There are other executives who were told or assumed that they would be reporting directly to the chief executive officer, only to learn that they would be reporting to the chief financial officer, chief operating officer, or an executive vice-president.

Then there is the guaranteed promotion to a position within a certain period of time that never materializes.

A typical provision would look like this:

> The Company hereby employs Employee and Employee hereby accepts such employment as chief executive officer of the Company with the title of Chief Executive Officer. As Chief Executive Officer, the Employee shall be the chief executive and operating officer of the Company and all other officers of the Company shall report to Employee, and the Employee shall perform such responsibilities, duties, and authority as set forth in the Company's bylaws and as are customarily assigned to such position. Employee shall perform his or her duties under the supervision and general direction of the Board of Directors. Employee agrees to diligently and conscientiously devote Employee's full and exclusive business time and attention, and his or her best efforts to discharge his or her duties in such capacity.

NEGOTIATION POINT # 1:

If the employee desires to have outside business activity, then such activity should be carved out in this provision of the employment agreement. For example, the employee may want to give speeches, teach courses, write articles and books, blog, do podcasts, do consulting work for a spouse's business, or create a start-up.

NEGOTIATION POINT # 2:

If the employee and the company have agreed that the executive is guaranteed a promotion, *e.g.*, to president, chief executive officer, chairman, *etc.*, then the title with position responsibilities and date of promotion should be included in this Position Title, Duties, and Responsibilities provision.

2　Term and Termination

Both the employer and the employee should know the contemplated initial term of the employment exactly: One year, three years, or five years? Also, the term and termination provision should make clear whether the term-end date is definite, or automatically renews at the term-end date with a new term of the same length of time, or renews based upon some notice mechanism. The termination provisions may be "with cause" or "without cause." Later in this chapter, we will discuss causes for termination and an executive's own ability to terminate unilaterally under certain conditions.

3　Base Salary/Compensation

Yearly base salary or base compensation should be set out in writing. It should be very straightforward. It is $200,000 or $1,000,000 or whatever. Intricate formulas usually appear in bonuses and profit sharing.

4 Bonuses: Incentive, Merit, Signing, and Retention

Many companies have elaborate bonus structures and the variations are unlimited. Signing bonuses and retention bonuses should also be straightforward. If a company does not offer a signing bonus, the executive should ask for one, especially when the executive is taking a risk or suffering an economic loss by switching employers.

It is important to understand the methodology of incentive or merit bonuses. The formulas can be quite complex and arcane. If you do not truly understand how it works, then ask the hiring contact to explain and keep asking until you do understand. If you are not confident in the explanation, then have a third party like an accountant, attorney, or benefits consultant take a look at it. If you cannot explain it to your significant other, then you do not truly understand the methodology.

5 Health Insurance, Supplemental Health Insurance, and Dental Insurance

Medical, dental, and vision insurance are expensive both for individual plans and family plans. Health care coverage definitely should be part of your calculation of the economic cost/benefit in moving to a new employer. Find out who the insurers are and how generous and expensive the plan will be. Do not wait for the human resources department packet to arrive after you have started the job. You may not like the coverage limitations and out-of-pocket expenses.

6   Pension Plan and Supplemental Retirement Plans/ 401(k) or 403(b)

A company's pension plan and benefits are going to be pretty much set in stone. You need to study them to understand the economic costs/ benefits of moving to the prospective employer.

7   Severance Pay

Severance pay is a big item to which you must pay attention and it must be addressed at the outset. An employee's being abruptly terminated with no future income can be catastrophic. The next chapter on separation agreements further addresses the topic of severance pay.

8   Vacation Days/Sick Days/Personal Days/ Holidays and Flexible Work Schedule

For many people, there is a trade-off between compensation and personal time off. If time off for personal or religious reasons is critical to you, then find out what the standard personal time off is for the company, and determine whether it meets your needs concerning vacation days, personal days, sick days, and religious holidays. If you desire to work only four 10-hour-long days a week (as opposed to five eight-hour-long days a week), or come in early and leave before five o'clock, or come in late and leave late, then the company's flexibility around those arrangements must be discussed. Also, telecommuting full or part time is becoming a more common option at many employers. You are in a better position to negotiate these arrangements before you start a job than afterward.

9 Life Insurance/Disability Insurance/Malpractice Insurance/Directors' and Officers' Insurance

Life insurance is pretty much standard for most large employers. Disability may or may not be available; however, you should inquire. Disability insurers say you are more likely to become disabled on the job than die on the job. I am not an actuary, so I cannot verify that claim, but it does not hurt to ask (pun intended). If you are a professional like an accountant, attorney, architect, or physician, you should confirm that the company has sufficient malpractice insurance that will cover you. As an officer, a director, or an executive, you need to confirm that the employer has "Directors' and Officers'" (D&O) coverage to protect you in case of claims arising from your performing your duties during the course of your employment. D&O coverage is revisited again later in this chapter in relation to the importance of an indemnification provision.

Other Items to Consider, If Applicable to Your Situation

- Marketing/entertainment expense account
- Continuing education
- Tuition reimbursement
- Automobile
- Moving expense and temporary housing allowance
- Permanent housing allowance; corporate apartment
- Parking
- Smartphone
- Computer/laptop/notebook
- Private dining club

- Clothing allowance
- Travel allowance for overseas postings
- Stock options
- Restricted stock (stock grants with vesting periods)
- No-interest company personal loans
- Support staff
- Office equipment and supplies
- Professional or trade association dues
- Professional license fees
- Corporate airplane
- Non-insurance covered medical costs
- Spousal travel allowance
- Tuition for private elementary and secondary schools for overseas postings

Terminations for Cause

Most executive employment agreements have termination-of-employee-for-cause provisions. The "causes" can range from misuse or misappropriation of money or property of a company, use of drugs or intoxicants, conduct that disparages the business integrity of the company or its officers or directors, employees, or customers, failure or refusal to perform a directive of a board of directors, conviction of a felony, conviction of a misdemeanor involving fraud, dishonest conduct, or a material breach of the employment agreement, restrictive covenants, or company policies. Termination for cause has adverse consequences for the executive in terms of reputation, future employability, and the loss of severance pay and benefits.

There are two key issues to keep in mind. First, the executive should ensure that there is due process in the company's determination of termination for cause and that it is not done within the sole discretion of the company. Second, language pertaining to turpitude and morals must be understood and eliminated or suitably qualified. Interesting fact: "moral turpitude" as a cause for termination is the most Google-referred search topic to my blog (www.yourexecutivelife.com). Go figure.

Termination for Cause: Moral Turpitude

When employment contracts have a termination-for-cause provision, it may include the term "moral turpitude." The following are two different examples of a termination-for-cause definition clause containing moral turpitude:

Example 1
Employee's conviction of, or guilty plea or *nolo contendere* plea to, or

confession of, a Class A-type felony or felony involving moral turpitude.

Example 2
Employee's conviction of, or plea of guilty or *nolo contendere* to,

a) a felony (other than traffic violations);

b) a crime involving moral turpitude; or

c) a criminal act which adversely affects the business or reputation of Company, its parent or its subsidiaries.

These typical for-cause termination clauses that use the term "moral turpitude" do not define the concept.

The term "turpitude" means vile, depraved, shameful, or base. It has a grave meaning, and even the sound of the word suggests perverseness. You add the word "moral" before "turpitude" and it suggests an egregiously bad act or immoral conduct. While we have a textbook definition of "moral turpitude" as being reprehensible conduct, what can it mean in practice? Who knows? However, an executive should care.

The term is too vague and subjective. Crimes come in varying degrees of wrongdoing. Felonies involve varying degrees of criminality. Some crimes are worse than others. In order to avoid arbitrary results and inconsistent employer or judicial application, we ought to discard this hidebound term altogether. When representing executives and professionals or organizations seeking to enter into employment contracts, I discourage the use of this term. I prefer an itemized list of causes for termination and plain language like the following clause:

> Employee's commission of any act (i) involving (A) misuse or misappropriation of money or other property of Corporation or (B) a felony or repeated use of drugs or intoxicants; or (ii) which disparages the business integrity of Corporation, its parent Corporation, or subsidiaries, or affiliates or their officer directors, employees, or customers, and materially and adversely affects the business reputation of Corporation.

This above sample clause makes it readily understandable, among other acts, what kind of crime would be cause for termination, *i.e.* a felony. In any jurisdiction, what constitutes a felony can be readily ascertained.[1] In the first two flawed moral turpitude clauses above, the term crime or felony is modified by the term "moral turpitude" and, consequently, makes the felony or crime vaguer and makes it more difficult to determine the applicability of the clause.

The use of the term moral turpitude is anachronistic and should be eliminated from employment contract termination-for-cause provisions.

Termination for Cause from Morals Clause

A morals clause is not to be confused with a moral turpitude provision.

Getting Booted for Behaving Badly

I grew up in Southern California and it was commonplace to hear about the lives and sometimes scandals of screen stars and entertainers, but I had never heard of "morals clauses." My first-year contracts course at the University of Michigan Law School did not cover this concept, so I was unfamiliar with this legal terminology. I was a newly minted lawyer when the term first entered my consciousness in the 1980s, because the then reigning Miss America, Vanessa Williams, became the subject of notoriety arising from *Penthouse* magazine publishing nude photos of her. Using a morals clause in its standard agreement with contestants, the Miss America Pageant took her crown away because of these nude photos. It was a big deal then; it may not be so controversial now.

As described earlier, "moral turpitude" is a related concept used in employment contracts for executives and professionals. Anything having to do with "morals" is always of interest to people, usually for prurient or judgmental reasons, but especially when it affects their own compensation.

Protecting an Organization's Brand

Morals clauses are most often used with entertainers and athletes. Companies desire to use celebrities as spokespersons or endorsers of the companies' products or services — think NBA stars or Olympic Gold Medal athletes on cereal boxes. Historically these clauses were directed at both criminal actions and socially disapproved behaviors reflecting the mores of the times.

As companies and organizations seek to enhance their brand, reputation, and goodwill, they also want the ability to protect those assets from damage arising from the personal actions or statements of their vendors, endorsers, consultants, spokespersons, partners, and employees.

Another example, National Football League Pittsburgh Steeler running back Rashard Mendenhall's Talent Agreement with Hanesbrands, Inc. contained the following morals clause:

> If Mendenhall commits or is arrested for any crime or becomes involved in any situation or occurrence... tending to bring Mendenhall into public disrepute, contempt, scandal, or ridicule, or tending to shock, insult, or offend the majority of the consuming public or any protected class or group thereof, then we shall have the right to immediately terminate this Agreement. HBI's decision on all matters arising under this Section...shall be conclusive.

Because of certain tweets by Mr. Mendenhall on Twitter concerning the death of Osama bin Laden, Hanesbrands, Inc. invoked the morals clause and terminated its Talent Agreement with Mendenhall, who then filed a breach of contract suit.

A consultant contract with which I was involved contained the following clause:

> The Company may terminate this Agreement without notice if Contractor is deemed to have engaged in misconduct, unethical behavior, or actions that disrupt or are inappropriate in the workplace.

The consultant would not have gotten the contract without agreeing to this clause.

A CEO employment contract had the following for-cause termination language:

> Any actions taken by Employee which in the sole opinion of the Company's Board of Directors materially adversely affects the business, goodwill, or reputation of the Company or its customers.

The CEO in this instance was able to negotiate away this broad, absolute language.

Personal Behavior and Private Actions

What we see here is a conflict between the right to engage in personal behavior and the right of the employer to protect its brand and reputation.

If one were the attorney for the employer, then one would want to expand the scope of these clauses to give the organizational client complete flexibility to control any potential or actual damages to its brand or to control any future direction of the brand.

If one were the attorney for the employee, consultant, or celebrity pitch person/endorser, then one would want to carve out as much right to personal action and privacy as possible and have more specificity of actionable behavior. The definition and application of morality can be vague, subjective, and arbitrary.

Meeting Halfway

If you take the King Solomon approach where there is an instance in which reasonable people could disagree as to the degree or appropriateness of the purported transgression (as determined by an arbitrator or mediator), then some lump sum payment to terminate the talent or employment agreement is probably the way to go.

It is only prudent for parties to spend ample time negotiating and crafting termination provisions — in particular the morals clause subsections of those provisions.

Firing the Employer

Executive employment agreements will ordinarily have termination of employment provisions. Executives will assume the termination provisions go one way, *i.e.* that the employer is always doing the terminating. What about the executive terminating his or her own employment?

Termination for Good Reason

Sophisticated executives or professionals will negotiate a provision that allows them to terminate their employment for "Good Reason" and still receive certain compensation and benefits from the employer. The provisions for termination for good reason by the executive can range from a few sentences to several paragraphs.

Categories of Good Reason

The employment agreement should define "Good Reason." Such a definition may include an event such as the assignment to the executive of any duties inconsistent in any material respect with the executive's position, duties, responsibilities, or status with the company as of the date of the employment agreement, or if a change in control has occurred, immediately prior to such change in control. It may include a change in the executive's reporting responsibilities, titles, or offices with the company. It may include any failure to re-elect the executive to any position with the company held by the executive. It may include a reduction of the executive's annual base salary. It may include any demand that the executive be based anywhere other than at the facility where the executive is currently located. It may include travel on company business to an extent substantially more burdensome than the ordinary travel requirements of the executive. It may include the failure of the company to continue in effect any employee benefit plan or compensation plan in which the executive is enrolled. It may include the failure of the company to continue to provide executive and executive's dependents medical, dental, disability, and life insurance benefits. It may include failure of the company to provide the executive with paid vacation. It could include failure to reimburse promptly the executive for any reasonable employment expenses.

Negotiating a Termination Clause

The events that could be deemed a Good Reason for an executive to terminate the employment agreement are numerous and varied. Like anything else, it is a matter for negotiation.

The more star power an executive has, coupled with a lack of need to take the position, the more leverage she has to negotiate her right to terminate with resulting substantial compensation and benefits. Of course, the prudent and professional executive early, clearly, and earnestly raises her concerns to resolve any issues that would lead the executive to initiate Good Reason termination.

NOTE WELL:

A wise executive controls the circumstances of his employment. An executive employee's right to fire his employer is a huge step in that direction.

Non-Compete

According to the English philosopher Francis Bacon, "A man must make his opportunity as oft as find it."

Preventing a person from making his opportunity runs counter to the American ethos that a person should have the freedom to work wherever and whenever that person desires. This notion has been tempered by contractual and equitable principles that a person can bargain away or limit his freedom to work under certain circumstances, as manifested in non-compete agreements (or covenants not to compete). Courts are loath to deprive someone of the ability to make a living. The following comments are a generic discussion of this kind of agreement or restrictive covenant.

Non-compete agreements are most often used in employment contracts and business purchase agreements. To be a valid contract, a non-compete agreement must be supported by "legal consideration,"[2] which means the price bargained for and paid for a promise (it may be a promise in return, an act, or a forbearance).

Most courts closely scrutinize non-compete agreements, as they are restraints on trade and considered to be contrary to public policy. A non-compete agreement is unenforceable where its sole purpose is to restrict competition without other justifying factors. Because there is more of an arm's-length bargaining position of the parties in non-compete agreements arising from the purchase of business assets, they are viewed more favorably by courts. A court will ordinarily sustain a non-compete agreement that is necessary to protect the promisee's legitimate proprietary or business interests.

The court's determination of the validity of a non-compete agreement is done by examining whether the terms are reasonable. The circumstances of each case will drive this determination. Reasonableness is measured by the scope of the territory, duration, the type of restricted activity, the hardship on the promising party, and the effect on the general public. The longer the duration and the larger the geographic territory, the more likely a court could find such terms as overbroad and contrary to public policy and, therefore, unenforceable.

The lack of any geographic limitation can be problematic, and without some legitimate qualifier on the prohibited activity placed on promisor, such as the promisor not soliciting particular existing customers of promisee, the covenant could be invalidated. Typically, non-compete agreements have a duration from six months to three years. In a sale-of-a-business situation, one court allowed five years, because the agreement did not prohibit the selling party from engaging in all business activity, just the kind of activities that competed with the business subject to the sale agreement.

To enforce a non-compete agreement, a promisee may seek an injunction against the promisor. Sometimes a promisor will file an action for declaratory judgment seeking to invalidate a non-compete agreement. Depending on the circumstances, monetary damages could be awarded, as well as attorneys' fees to the prevailing party.

At a time of new possibilities and opportunities, an executive who is considering moving to another company should carefully scrutinize her non-compete agreement, as well as the non-solicitation and confidentiality agreements with her current employer, to ascertain whether by moving to the new company the executive would be in violation. The executive should not try to do this without the assistance of legal counsel. Employers have gotten more aggressive about seeking enforcement of these agreements, as evidenced by the burgeoning court cases around the country.

Non-Solicitation

Non-solicitation provisions in employment contracts are very common. This restrictive covenant aims to prevent an existing or former employee from soliciting customers, clients, employees, vendors, and suppliers of the existing or former employer. The prohibition on soliciting of customers and clients is to prevent losing business from existing clients and customers with whom the employee has established a relationship while working for the employer. The prohibition on soliciting employees of the employer is to prevent losing talent to a competing business. There is usually a post-employment restricted period, two years for instance, in which the departed employee cannot solicit. Sometimes a retroactive time period of applicability is included, for example those customers with whom the employee has interacted in the last three years. The scope of applicability can be as broad as to include any prospective customer that has been pitched or cultivated by the company. Whether a particular court will enforce such a broad non-solicitation covenant cannot be predicted.

A typical non-solicitation provision will look like this:

> Employee agrees that during the Restricted Period, he will not directly or indirectly (A) solicit the trade of, or trade with, any customer, prospective customer, or supplier of the Company for any business purpose other than for the benefit of the Company or (B) solicit or induce, or attempt to solicit or induce, any employee, director or vendor or supplier of the Company to leave the Company for any reason whatsoever or hire any employee, director, vendor or supplier of the Company.

LinkedIn and Non-Compete and Non-Solicitation Agreements

Lawsuits have resulted from LinkedIn communications bumping up against employment restrictive covenants.

People have gotten way too comfortable with social media such as Facebook, Twitter, Instagram, and LinkedIn. We forget two important things: that what is sent into the Internet never really goes away, and that it can be conceivably be read by thousands, if not millions of individuals. Most disturbingly, much of it can be used in a court of law as evidence against you.

Merely updating your profile on LinkedIn to announce your new employment position to all your connections that you developed in your previous job, especially to those contacts that also happen to be current customers or clients of your previous employer, could prompt a lawsuit from the old employer. Also, depending upon how broad and aggressive the non-solicitation clause is, the LinkedIn announcement could be deemed as a solicitation that violates such a non-solicitation clause. A screen shot of the LinkedIn update could be Exhibit "A" of the complaint filed by the employer.

Mere announcement may not be enough, but LinkedIn in-mail solicitation of former employer customers and clients could fall within the non-compete and non-solicitation clauses' parameters. Your operating in certain restricted geographic areas and communicating with specific customers of the former employer could get you an adverse verdict in court.

Whether a LinkedIn update or message communication to one's contacts will constitute a breach of non-solicitation and non-compete provisions will be driven by the facts of the particular case. Bad facts can land a former employee or her new employer in hot water.

The medium of communication, whether it is telephone, e-mail, mail, fax, or social media, does not change the substance of improper communication that may violate non-solicitation, confidentiality, and non-compete provisions.

Finally, social media is still an evolving world of communication that must be approached prudently. One must be conscious of the social, legal, and business impacts of whatever messages and images one is putting on the Internet.

Non-Solicitation Covenant Versus Non-Compete Covenant

In terms of restrictive covenants, I believe the real meat lies in the covenant not to solicit customers. In my view, the non-solicitation covenant has more impact than a non-compete covenant. This is so for two reasons: the non-compete covenant is more vulnerable to legal attack, and the non-solicitation covenant can be more specifically tailored to protecting the legitimate business interests of the company by identifying the company's true existing customers with whom the departing employee would not have developed a relationship "but for" his employment with his company.

A well drafted non-solicitation covenant can make a non-compete covenant superfluous.

A judge who has problems with an unreasonable non-compete provision may carry over his or her skepticism and displeasure to other legitimate, reasonable restrictive covenants like non-solicitation.

Confidentiality and Intellectual Property Provisions

Confidentiality and Non-Disclosure Provisions

Confidentiality provisions in employment contracts have become pretty standard. Because of the boom in technology in the last three decades, there is a lot more intellectual property and proprietary information to be protected.

Neither the employer nor the employee should underestimate the utility of confidentiality and non-disclosure provisions. Proprietary business information is a critical, but underappreciated, asset of many companies. For example, in Illinois, the Trade Secrets Act protects a company's information that is treated as secret and has economic value because it is not generally known to other persons. This information includes technical or nontechnical data, a formula, a pattern, compilation, program, device, method, technique, drawing, process, financial data, or list of actual or potential customers or suppliers. A confidentiality agreement protects the employer's trade secrets and informs the employee what information is permissible for him to utilize post-employment.

It's Not Secret If Everyone Knows About It or Employees Don't Know It's a Secret

Confidentiality Agreements are meant to protect the proprietary information and trade secrets of a business. If the executive leadership has not instituted safeguards, controls, and notices of confidentiality for its important business information, then do not expect a court readily to treat it as confidential information.

An employee confidentiality agreement is a good start. Physical and technological protections of business information, along with legal protection of intellectual property through copyrights and patents, are a good finish. Think locked filing cabinets, password-protected computer files, documents marked "confidential," and so forth. It is never too early or too late to establish protocols for safeguarding trade secrets and other company information.

Carve-Outs

I cannot say this enough: If you already have pre-existing relationships with employees, customers, clients, potential customers, and potential clients, then be sure to list those in a carve-out provision before you sign non-solicitation, non-compete, and confidentiality agreements; there may be overlap between your existing contacts and your prospective employer's contacts and you do not want to be precluded from utilizing them post-employment.

In turn, employers should remind departing employees that their social media may not be used as an end-run around any restrictions contained in confidentiality, non-solicitation, and non-compete agreements.

Inventions

Employers of all types, not just technology companies, will want to establish their rights to all discoveries, inventions, improvements, and innovations arising from an employee's work for the business or organization. Whether the employee's work is patentable or not, copyrightable or not, or trademarkable or not, the employer will seek ownership rights. The inventions provision may cover only those things created on company time or using company resources, or it may also include those things not created on company time or using company resources if they pertain to the employer's business. The inventions provision will require the employee to disclose her inventions and to assign her interest to the employer and execute any other documents necessary to protect and perfect the employer's interest in the invention, innovation or creation.

Although they can vary in length from three sentences to two pages, an assignment of intellectual property provision typically looks like the following:

> ASSIGNMENT OF INVENTIONS. I agree that I will promptly make full written disclosure to the Company, will hold in trust for the sole right and benefit of the Company, and hereby assign to the Company, or its designee, all my right, title, and interest in and to any and all inventions, original works of authorship, developments, concepts,

> improvements, designs, discoveries, ideas, trade-
> marks or trade secrets, whether or not patentable or
> registrable under copyright or similar laws, which I
> may solely or jointly conceive or develop or reduce
> to practice, or cause to be conceived or developed
> or reduced to practice, during the period of time I am
> in the employ of the Company.

The employee should understand at the time of signing an agreement that much of the intellectual capital and information he or she
creates for the company may not go along with him or her when he or
she leaves the company. Where the employee has been developing an
idea or invention prior to being offered a position with a new employer,
he or she should specifically carve out that idea or invention from the
assignment agreement.

Copyrights

I Wrote It, So Why Can't I Use It?

You are leaving your job or you have already left. After you leave, you
want to use all of your PowerPoint presentations, white papers, news-
letter articles, and blog posts that you did for your employer. Not so
fast. Are you allowed to do that? Who owns the written work that you
produced? Increasingly I am called to advise incoming or departing
executives and professionals on how to preserve and protect their
intellectual property rights or understand how to avoid violating the
intellectual property rights of their former employers.

You need to know the copyright laws. You also need to know what
confidentiality/intellectual property agreements you may have signed,
either in an employment agreement or in a separation/severance agreement, or both.

The basics for a copyright are:

- A work must be original.

- A work must be completed and in tangible form, like a written article.

- A copyright holder has the right to reproduce, to distribute, and to modify the work, and to perform or display it.

- A copyright holder neither has to register his\her\its work to gain copyright protection nor has to display the copyright symbol.

An employee should note well that ordinarily the employee's work authored within the defined scope of the employee's employment constitutes a "work made for hire." Although the employee physically created the work, the employee may not own it, but rather the employer does. As noted previously, most savvy employers will eliminate any legal ambiguity about copyright ownership by having the employee sign intellectual property and invention assignment agreements.

Again, it cannot be over emphasized that prior to commencing employment, an employee would do well to carve out in a written agreement any existing invention, original works of authorship, and so on, to ensure such work product or invention is not assigned to or deemed owned by the employee's new employer. Also, prior to any departure, the employee should set out in an agreement what works the employee created that were not created on the job or are not assigned to the company.

When the employee does not own the written work that the employee created, the most obvious and practical thing to do is simply ask permission from the previous employer.

Lastly, there is a limited way to use copyrighted material without permission and not infringe. This way is called "fair use." For example, if you fairly and reasonably use a short quote and credit it for commentary and criticism, news reporting, teaching, research or parody, you are probably okay. The evaluation includes whether your use adversely affects the market for or value of the work. When in doubt, consult an attorney.

Non-Compete, Non-Solicitation, and Confidentiality Take-Aways

Five things to note:

1. Carve out from your non-compete, non-solicitation, and confidentiality provisions those clients, customers, relationships, and contacts that you acquired at your previous employers; there may be overlap between your existing contacts and your prospective employer's contacts and you do not want to be precluded from utilizing them post-employment.

2. An executive should consult an attorney to analyze his or her non-compete agreement for potential breach prior to accepting a new position.

3. Executives and their new employers are now more willing to challenge non-compete provisions through litigation.

4. Spurned old employers will often seek to enforce non-compete agreements through litigation.

5. You should not be lulled by the false sense of intimacy and instant camaraderie of social media like LinkedIn and Facebook. Our communications, whether on the Internet or face to face, can have unanticipated legal consequences.

Non-Disparagement Covenant

Non-disparagement provisions are not just found in separation/severance agreements when an employee is terminated. These provisions can also be found in employment agreements when an executive is being hired. A careful employer would use a belt-and-suspenders approach and have a non-disparagement covenant in both the employment agreement and the separation agreement the employer makes with the executive. So, too, the executive would be prudent to negotiate non-disparagement provisions in the executive's employment agreement and executive's separation agreement. Brand protection is critical to the employer's business, and reputation management is key to the executive's career.

A typical non-disparagement provision in an employment agreement would look something like the following:

> NON-DISPARAGEMENT. During the Employee's employment by the Company and after the Employee's termination of employment for any reason, Employee agrees not to make any adverse or disparaging comments (written or oral) about the Company or any of its respective, officers, directors, stockholders, managers, or employees which may tend to impugn or injure any of their reputation, goodwill, and relationships with their past, present, or future investors, customers, employees, or vendors, or with the business community or the media generally. In addition, during the

Employee's employment by the Company and after the Employee's termination of employment for any reason, the Company agrees not to make any adverse or disparaging comments (written or oral) about the Employee which may tend to impugn or injure his or her reputation, goodwill, and relationships with past, present, or future customers, employers, or vendors, or with the business community or the media generally. Nothing in this Section is intended to prohibit, limit, or prevent either party from providing truthful testimony in a court of law, to a regulatory or law enforcement agency, or pursuant to a properly issued subpoena, and such testimony would not be deemed to be a violation of this Section.

NEGOTIATION POINT:

A non-disparagement provision applicable to both parties should be a non-negotiable included provision.

We will revisit non-disparagement in Chapter Two.

Liquidated Damages Provision

A liquidated-damages clause is a "contractual provision that determines in advance the measure of damages if a party breached the agreement." *Black's Law Dictionary* 949 (8th Edition 2004). The benefit can be that the difficulty and necessity of calculating and proving damages in court or arbitration are avoided.

Recently, I saw a spate of news articles about a TV broadcast company that routinely utilized liquidated damages clauses in its employment contract. The company's use of liquidated damages clauses intrigued me because I rarely come across liquidated damages clauses when reviewing or drafting employment contracts for clients.

Objectively, it is a strategic tool in an employer's employment contract box to protect its legitimate business interests. Generally, its enforceability will be driven by the particular facts of employment, the reasonableness of the agreed-upon damages, and the language of the particular provision.

Its apparently controversial use by the company prompted me to review my ample employment agreement files to assess the extent liquidated damages clauses were used. I did find a couple of them in two fields: media talent and physicians.

As I represent both employers and employees, depending on the particular client — employer or employee — I would advocate for or against such a clause on behalf of that client.

Although liquidated damages could be onerous for an employee, other clauses like non-compete, non-solicitation, confidentiality, payment of prevailing party's attorney's fees if party loses in litigation, and out-of-town and mandatory arbitration, among other clauses, can be just as problematic for an employee.

I cannot be too sympathetic to employees who are penny wise and pound foolish in not paying for an employment lawyer to negotiate better employment agreement provisions for them including liquidated damages. It is akin to "buyer's remorse" and the employee can only look to himself for signing an unsatisfactory employment contract.

An employer has the right to protect its business interests and an employee has the right to advance his or her own economic and legal interests. Everything is negotiable.

You may want to know what exactly makes up a liquidated damages provision in a contract. Although not ordinarily seen in employment contracts, they are frequently used in commercial and real estate contracts.

The law concerning liquidated damages may vary depending upon the state. Using Illinois as an example, its courts state that as "a general rule of contract law that, for reasons of public policy, a liquidated damages clause which operates as a penalty for nonperformance or as a threat to secure performance will not be enforced." Jameson Realty Group v. Kostiner, 351 Ill. App. 3d 416, 423 (2004).

However, Illinois courts will uphold the validity and enforceability of a liquidated damages provision when it meets three elements:

1. the parties intended to agree in advance to the settlement of damages that might arise from the breach;

2. the amount of liquidated damages was reasonable at the time of contracting, bearing some relation to the damages which might be sustained; and

3. the actual damages would be uncertain in amount and difficult to prove. Jameson, at 423.

A proposed liquidated damages clause in an employment contract could read something like this:

> If Talent leaves the company before the end of Talent's Employment term except for reasons set forth above in Section __ of this agreement, Talent agrees to pay on demand to Employer one-half (1/2) of Talent's annual salary as liquidated damages and not as a penalty, and the parties agree that such amount constitutes a reasonable provision for liquidated damages.

This fictional provision is an amalgam of two employment contracts that contained proposed liquidated damage clauses. Now whether it would be acceptable to an employee is another matter. Again, whether this particular fictional provision would be enforceable will depend on the particular facts and the particular state jurisdiction.

Of course, such a provision is put forth by the employer as a disincentive to the employee from leaving the employer before the end of the employment term or from violating a restrictive covenant like a noncompete clause. It is up to the employee and employee's attorney to negotiate the elimination or reduction of the liquidated damages amount.

Mandatory Arbitration Clauses in Employment Agreements

In employment contract negotiations, employers and employees often focus on different points and have different priorities. One typical provision where the parties may diverge in their hierarchy of important negotiating points is the mandatory arbitration clause, arbitration being an alternative to litigation for resolving disputes.

Arbitration clauses are not necessarily standard in every employment agreement, but their significance should not be discounted. Parties need to pay attention to them. Employers generally favor them because of the time, expense, and unpredictability of litigation. Courts are increasingly willing to enforce mandatory arbitration clauses involving employment disputes, including discrimination rights claims. Although an arbitration process ordinarily will not have the expensive, expanded discovery process and extensive motions phase that occur in civil litigation, the arbitration hearing itself can be as expensive as a trial.

Under mandatory arbitration, the arbitrator's decision is final and binding and enforceable in any court of competent jurisdiction. The arbitrator is obviously supposed to be neutral and may or may not have familiarity with or expertise in the subject matter. Arbitration proceedings are much less formal than the legal rules and procedures of a court and the arbitrator may receive and consider evidence that may not pass muster in a court of law. Because arbitration is a cousin of mediation, the arbitrator may be more inclined to split the baby, so to speak, rather than to make a draconian up-or-down, win-lose decision. By choosing arbitration, an employer can usually avoid the risk of a runaway jury or a plaintiff-employee-prone judge.

An important consideration for the employee is that in the arbitration clause, the employer will designate the location of the arbitration hearing, which may not be in a locale that is near the employee. If the hearing is required to be in Chicago, but the employee lives in Los Angeles, then that will be inconvenient and expensive for the employee.

Done fairly, arbitration can be helpful to both employer and employee.

NOTE WELL:

As far as alternative dispute resolution forums go, *mediation*, I believe, is a more cost-effective, less onerous way to go for both employer and employee. Mediation is an informal, confidential negotiation process to achieve resolution of a dispute. This process is facilitated by an independent, neutral third party. Both employer and employee should push for a mediation provision. Some agreements will have a three-step process: first mediation, then arbitration, and then litigation.

Choice of Governing Law and Forum Selection Provisions in Employment Contracts

Most employment contracts will have provisions that dictate that the contract will be governed by the laws of a particular state ("choice of law") and that litigation, if any, must take place in a certain state, California, for instance ("forum selection"). These provisions are often overlooked entirely or given short shrift in the employment contract review process. That is a big mistake.

Choice of Law (Governing Law)

Generally, the basic limitations on enforcing a choice of law provision are that there must be some relationship between the transaction that is the subject of the agreement and the selected jurisdiction or that there is some other reasonable basis for the choice of law of the selected jurisdiction.

Forum Selection

Forum selection dictates the location of the court that shall adjudicate the parties' disputes arising from a contract. Forum selection provisions are *prima facie* valid. As parties are free to contract, again, generally, the enforceability of a forum selection provision becomes a matter of its reasonableness and it not being against public policy.

Employer Drives Choice of Law and Forum Selection

An employer will usually designate the state in which it is headquartered for both choice of law and the location where a lawsuit concerning the contract may be physically brought. For many employers, these are reflexive choices because they believe the forum for litigation in their headquartered state is more convenient for them.

The lawyer for the employer is usually admitted to practice law in the state in which the employer is headquartered and, therefore, the lawyer is most familiar and comfortable with contract, labor and other laws of that state. However, an examination of the "home state" laws may reveal that some or all of these laws may actually be more favorable to the employee. For example, if we look at non-compete provisions that are found in many employment contracts, some states' courts are more liberal than others in enforcing them. Some other state courts have a stricter standard in upholding the enforceability of non-competes because these courts frown on restraints that prevent an individual from being able to earn a livelihood.

Friendly Forum

Some states are friendlier toward individual plaintiffs and less friendly toward large corporations involved in litigation against individuals. Even certain counties within a particular state may be more or less friendly toward individual plaintiffs or defendants; therefore a corporate party may even seek to designate a specific county. Employees are more likely to negotiate for a forum closest to where they live, as litigating a lawsuit 1,000 miles away may be cost prohibitive.

So the selection of forum can be a very important decision for either the employer or the employee.

Indemnification and D&O Insurance in Employment Contracts

Indemnification by Employer

In my law practice covering executive employment contracts, I see too infrequently a provision requiring an employer to indemnify an executive for any costs, expenses, liabilities, and losses incurred by the executive in the performance of his duties with the company. Usually, the indemnification arises in the context of litigation costs. It should apply to any kind of claim or proceeding, including an action, lawsuit, arbitration, investigation, or administrative proceeding. It should also apply to both civil and criminal actions, investigations, and proceedings.

The costs, expenses, liabilities, and losses should include, but not be limited to, reasonable attorneys' fees, judgments, interest, expenses of investigation, fines, excise taxes or penalties, and amounts paid or to be paid by executive in any settlement.

A well-drafted indemnification provision will require the employer to advance to the executive all his costs and expenses concerning a claim or proceeding.

An indemnification provision may have qualifying language that, as a precondition for indemnification, the executive must be properly performing his obligations in good faith.

Claw-Back of Indemnification Payments

Some indemnification provisions will have a mechanism that allows the employer to claw back the amounts advanced to an Executive if a determination has been made that the Executive was not entitled to indemnification for the subject costs and expenses.

The most comprehensive indemnification provision I have seen used reads as follows:

> Employee shall be held harmless and fully indemnified by Employer to the fullest extent permitted by [State X] law without qualification or limitation.

A companion provision that would be prudent for the executive to include in his employment agreement is that the employer be required to keep in place directors' and officers' ("D&O") liability insurance coverage for the executive during his employment with the employer and for four years afterward. An executive could be a designated officer of an entity. Generally, an officer owes fiduciary duties to his employer entity — like a corporation. These fiduciary duties encompass duty of care and duty of loyalty. An executive who is an officer should consult his employer's legal counsel about his obligations and potential liabilities arising from fiduciary duties. It is enough to say here that D&O insurance coverage must be evaluated and not overlooked.

Executives get investigated, prosecuted, and sued all the time. Having indemnification and D&O insurance provisions will offer the executive some peace of mind.

Indemnification by Employee

Employers sometimes require an executive to indemnify the company.

One kind of executive's obligation to indemnify involves the executive's indemnifying, defending, and holding her company harmless from any uninsured portion of any claim, loss, or expense arising from any action by the executive that contravenes the rules and policies of the company, or any applicable laws, or that arises from intentional misconduct by the executive.

New Employer's Protection from Old Employer's Restrictive Covenants

Another kind of executive's obligation to indemnify involves the executive warranting that said executive is not under any legal or contractual obligations that contravene the new employer's employment agreement, and execution of the employment agreement will not breach any other agreement by the executive. If there is such a breach, then the executive must indemnify the new employer and must hold the new employer harmless from and against any and all loss, damage, and expense emanating from the claim against the executive or the new employer arising from the executive's relationship with his previous employer. The breaches would typically involve non-compete provisions, non-solicitation provisions, and confidentiality provisions.

Employers must protect themselves from new employees who know they have valid legal obligations to previous employers, like confidentiality agreements. One additional way to protect themselves is for the employers to require the prospective employee to provide copies of all sections of employment and separation agreements containing restrictive covenants like non-compete, non-solicitation, and confidential information.

Employers should also be able to be made whole from the bad conduct of their employees giving rise to uninsured liability, like fraud.

The scope and kind of indemnification by an employee must be appropriately negotiated by each side. Obviously, indemnification amounts can be quite burdensome and even financially catastrophic for an employee.

The Silent Employment Contract Provision: The Implied Covenant of Good Faith and Fair Dealing

Sometimes it is necessary to state the obvious: An employment agreement is a contract that is subject to basic contract principles, interpretation, and construction.

Good Faith and Fair Dealing Required

We will often see in an employment agreement express covenants not to compete and not to solicit. What is not expressed in contracts, but implied in the law in many states, is the covenant of good faith and fair dealing. For example, Illinois law reads a duty of good faith and fair dealing into all contracts. The duty is implied in every contract. Employment agreements are no exception.

What does "good faith" and "fair dealing" mean? The idea is that whatever contractual discretion a party has, the party must exercise such discretion reasonably and not capriciously or arbitrarily. Good faith is not taking an opportunistic advantage that was not contemplated by the parties when they entered into their agreement.

Not Playing Nice

An act of bad faith could be where an employer having some discretion under a for-cause termination provision, terminates an employee arbitrarily or capriciously for allegedly disreputable behavior. Or it could be where an employer terminates an employee to avoid a payment deadline for stock vesting or bonus payment. An employee example could be where an employee makes her employment contingent on her spouse finding a similar job in the new locale as the employee, but the employee and her spouse purposely fail to obtain a new job because the employee has a change of heart and does not want to move.

In short, it is a matter of a fair, honest, and sincere course of dealing where the parties have some discretion.

Bulletproof Your Agreement by Expressing Yourself

Courts cannot use the implied covenant of good faith and fair dealing to override an express term of an agreement. Nor does this implied covenant ordinarily create a separate cause of action. The courts use the covenant as an aid to interpretation and construction. A well-drafted, comprehensive agreement should not fall victim to this implied covenant.

Without express disavowal in the employment agreement, the implied covenant exists. Accordingly, one party, who believes the other party is engaging in sharp practices by exploiting gaps in the employment agreement, may try to invoke the covenant.

CHAPTER TWO

THE END HAS COME:
THE SEPARATION AGREEMENT,
POST-EMPLOYMENT ACTIONS
AND CONSIDERATIONS

To Give Severance Payments or Not to Give, That Is the Question

Severance payments are pragmatic. Employers ought to consider allowing for severance payment and neutral letter-of-reference provisions in their separation agreements where there is no employee misconduct. These provisions often generate goodwill from a departing employee, thereby reducing lawsuits. The payment provisions can also be used to bind an employee to confidentiality, non-disparagement, non-solicitation and non-compete obligations as well as release employer of most of its actual or potential liabilities. Severance payments demonstrate humaneness and compassion on the part of the employer. Employers usually underestimate the destructive power that an angry, committed terminated employee can have on the morale, reputation, and resources of the organization.

What many employers fail to understand in not being reasonable in their severance offer is that the terminated, complaining employee may present a sympathetic image to a third-party fact finder in terms of discrimination charges concerning age, gender, religion, race, disability, and other issues. Inchoate (and sometimes manufactured) discrimination charges may rise to the surface for the first time when an employee feels he is not receiving a fair severance package.

The peeved employee may dig up bones of legal and regulatory liability of which the organization's higher-ups may not be aware. The organization may thus unintentionally spawn a whistle-blower.

Employment lawsuits are expensive and generate bad public relations for a company. As long as the severance compensation is not excessive, it really is a no-brainer to just pay it out in terms of a cost-benefit trade-off for an employer. What constitutes an appropriate severance payment will depend on one or more of the following factors: the industry, the amount of time employed with the employer and the level of the employee. Some companies have rigid formulas or policies for severance payments. These prescribed payments can range anywhere from the same lump sum for every terminated employee to one week for every year of service. Despite a company's so-called standard severance payment, the employee and her attorney should treat the severance payment as a negotiable amount. Every employer's circumstance and disposition will be different.

Understand the Condition of the Newly Fired

People who have never been terminated either by being laid off or by being fired have no idea of the shock, pain, embarrassment, and humiliation that a terminated executive or professional undergoes. I represent as many terminating employers as terminated executives, so I have a two-sided perspective on the process, the issues, conditions, mechanics, and, yes, the drama of it all. There are some executives who have never failed at anything. They have always gotten "straight-As" in school, were always first to be picked on a team on the playground, gotten great evaluations, received regular bonuses, and were promoted on the fast track. Many times terminations have nothing to do with the competency or productivity or even the personality of the fired executives. It could be a host of subjective reasons ranging from a boss's insecurities to favoritism to ageism to the assemblage of a "new team," and so forth. It could be for objective reasons like a bad economy, trimming expenses, or the need for different skill sets. Whatever the reason, getting fired hurts.

Stages of Loss

Getting fired is like losing a loved one and mimics the five stages of grief for diagnosed terminally ill patients as articulated by Elisabeth Kubler-Ross in her book *On Death and Dying*:

- Denial and isolation

- Anger

- Bargaining

- Depression

- Acceptance

A fired executive may experience one or more of these stages, in any sequence.

No Pity Parties and How to Depart from an Employer

Terminated executives ought to let themselves go through the grieving process for no more than two or three days, and then get over it. People get terminated all the time and the executive is not special for having been terminated. If you read the financial press, you know that the shelf-life of C-suite executives is getting shorter and shorter. Of course, losing one's job is a very unpleasant feeling, to say the least, but no one has a monopoly on adversity.

The sooner the executive begins working on his next great opportunity and not fixating on "what happened to me and why me," the better. It may be a cliché, but an executive's determination to have an optimistic attitude in his job quest does make a huge difference in reaching a successful outcome. More clichés: One should not burn any bridges with one's old employer and one should get busy as a beaver building new bridges to a new employer. An executive must race on to his next opportunity.

When leaving her employer, the executive or professional should do so on a positive note. If circumstances permit, the executive or professional should send out an e-mail announcement that is positive, forward-looking and concise. Any kind of communication with co-workers, customers, vendors, and third parties should maintain an upbeat theme. By doing this, the executive will accomplish three things:

1. generate goodwill and encourage the employer to help her and not hurt her, for instance, when it comes to references or a job search;

2. project confidence and teamwork on the executive's part; and

3. make the executive feel and look dignified and like a class act, thus boosting her own morale.

In short, no one wants to deal with a sourpuss or a "victim." Cheerfulness and positivity go a long way.

If a general announcement is to be sent out by the employer, the executive or professional should request to have input on the script. Ideally, the content of the script should include the executive's contributions, his teamwork, and his congeniality.

Sense of Entitlement

Terminated employees usually overestimate what they are "entitled to" and what the company would be willing to pay in severance payments and benefits. Unrealistic expectations lead to disappointment and deadlocked or terminated negotiations.

A company will have a severance payment number it deems economical, or sometimes a rigid severance calculation policy. An employee must understand that, without an employment contract severance payment provision, the company, rightly or wrongly, believes that it is doing the employee "a favor" by voluntarily giving the employee severance when the employee is legally entitled to nothing.

Run, Don't Walk, to Seek Advice of Counsel

Although separation agreements ordinarily admonish the employee to obtain legal counsel to review the separation agreement, too many employees drop the ball. The employee may fail to obtain legal counsel. The employee might tender the agreement to his attorney a couple of days before the drop-dead date for signature, leaving little time for a comprehensive legal review of the agreement and the employee's legal situation, and insufficient time to negotiate with the employer.

For some employees, the failure to obtain legal counsel is a cost-saving measure, which is being penny wise and pound foolish. For other employees, it is due to a lack of sophistication. For still others, it is because of their utter demoralization, resulting in passivity. Those employees represented by counsel more often negotiate better agreements than those who are not. Squeaky wheels get the grease.

OBSERVATION:

I have seen that those employees who remain passive and do not retain an advocate to act on their behalves become disgusted with themselves for their inaction for years to come.

For Employers: Non-Solicitation, Non-Compete, and Non-Disparagement Covenants Should Be *De Rigueur* in Separation Agreements

These covenants are covered in Chapter One. A reminder: There are distinctions that amount to substantial differences between **Non-Solicitation Covenants** and **Non-Compete Covenants.**

Non-Disparagement Appears Again

As we noted in Chapter One, non-disparagement covenants are more often seen in separation agreements than in employment agreements.

Many executives and professionals will face termination of employment in their careers. Termination may result from a firing, a lay-off, or a voluntary resignation. Frequently, a separation agreement with severance provisions will be part of the termination. Whatever the reason for termination, one often overlooked provision in the separation/severance documents is a non-disparagement provision. Both executive and employer may inadvertently omit this critical provision.

From the employer side, the employer does not want a disgruntled former executive trashing the company, thereby diminishing the brand, reputation, and goodwill of the company. The executive certainly does not want her ability to find new employment to be precluded by negative comments being made about her by personnel at her old employer.

In agreeing to a non-disparagement provision, the employer has to be careful in limiting the number of persons who would fall under the application of the non-disparagement provision. Obvious persons such as the C-suite executives and the board of directors and the HR Director could be controlled. The provision just as obviously should not apply to everyone in a company with 10,000 employees.

The scope of the application to the employee is much easier, as the employee should be able to control himself and his spouse.

Many times the non-disparagement provision is missing from the separation agreement and, if there is one, it usually is one-sided in favor of the employer.

When I recommend a non-disparagement provision to a client, whether an employer or an employee, I invariably get a why-didn't-I-think-of-that response.

From a risk management perspective, it is a way for employers to reduce defamation and libel lawsuits.

In most cases, a non-disparagement provision is a win-win in an executive termination.

NEGOTIATION POINT:

In order to expand the scope of non-disparagement by the employee to the employee's spouse, the employer could have the employee's spouse be a signatory to the non-disparagement provision and pay the spouse a nominal sum to establish "legal consideration"[3] for the agreement. Alternatively or additionally, the employer could have a claw-back severance payment penalty if the spouse has been found to have disparaged the former employer.

Non-Disparagement's Cousin — Defamation

"According to Solomon, life and death are in the power of the tongue; and as Euripides truly affirmeth, every unbridled tongue in the end shall find itself unfortunate…"

~Sir Walter Raleigh

Have you ever wondered why most Human Resources Departments are adamant in keeping to a bare minimum the information they give out concerning a former employee's reference checks? The information given is usually limited to dates of employment and titles of positions held. Salary and compensation information is rarely and only reluctantly given, even when there is a written authorization and release signed by the ex-employee. The HR people's reluctance is for good reason: avoidance of defamation lawsuits and privacy violation claims.

You Said What?

A couple of lawsuits involving defamation claims by executives are good reminders for employers that the involuntary or voluntary departure of executives must be done in a way that does not injure the reputation of the executive by anything that the employer says or writes.

In one case, a consulting firm's managing director telephoned a client to say that the consulting firm's former employee who was going to do work for the client was in a lawsuit with the consulting firm because the ex-employee "violated her non-compete agreement." Saying the former employee "violated her non-compete" could turn out to be defamatory. An appellate court reversed the lower court's dismissal of the ex-employee's claims of defamation and held "The alleged defamatory statement was alleged with particularity, was not substantially true as a matter of law, was not reasonably subject to an innocent construction, and was not subject to the fair report privilege." Huron Consulting Services LLC v. Murtha, et al., Appellate Court of Illinois (1st Judicial District 2012).

In another court case, an executive did prevail in his defamation suit against an individual member of his former company's supervisory board and against his former company. In that case, the board member walked into the president's office and fired him. The fired president called in a human resources employee as a witness and asked the firing board member to state his reasons for the firing. The firing board member replied, "for cause," and further answered "yes" to the president's query: "You are telling me that you are firing me for gross insubordination, for gross misconduct, for gross negligence and willful violation of the law?" Leyshon v. Diel Controls North America, Inc. *et al.*, Appellate Court of Illinois (1st Judicial District 2011). The Leyshon court stated, "It was a reasonable inference from the evidence at trial that plaintiff's termination for cause had become public knowledge and prevented the plaintiff from obtaining comparable employment." This appellate court upheld a jury award of $2,000,000 in compensatory damages and $6,000,000 in punitive damages. Ouch!

What is Defamation?

A statement becomes defamatory when it injures a person's reputation. The three elements of a defamation claim are 1) the statement is false, 2) the statement is made in an unprivileged publication to a third party, and 3) the publication damages the plaintiff.

Where a statement is defamatory *per se*, a plaintiff need not plead or prove damages to plaintiff's injury to her reputation. For example, Illinois law has five categories of defamatory *per se* statements:

1. those imputing the commission of a crime;

2. those imputing infection with a communicable disease;

3. those imputing an inability to perform or want of ethics in the discharge of duties of office or employment;

4. those that prejudice a party's trade, profession, or business, or impute lack of ability in the party's trade, profession, or business; and

5. those imputing fornication or adultery.

Accordingly, making statements about an employee's inability to perform, lack of integrity, or lack of ability in his trade, profession, or business without substantial evidence of its truth can land an employer and its management in very hot water.

If an employer is going to fire someone "for cause," the employer better have good factual documentation establishing cause and be careful to whom such information is told. As the Leyshon case discussed above shows, an employer would be foolish to use "for cause" as a subterfuge to avoid severance payments required under an employment contract. Unless the executive's conduct is so egregious that paying severance is not a public relations option, it may be better not to state a reason and simply pay in exchange for an appropriate release agreement.

If an employer has a non-compete claim, a non-solicitation claim, and/or a breach of confidentiality claim against an employee, it is best to let the lawsuit speak for itself. If the employer feels compelled to say anything to third parties, then it should be simply that there is a lawsuit alleging these claims that is of public record. To state that an alleged violation is "fact" leaves the employer vulnerable to a lawsuit and possible liability. The best employer statement to make is "No comment."

TAKE-AWAYS:

For the employer, the lesson is that any departure of an employee must be tightly managed so that no one in the company makes a disparaging statement about the employee that could result in a defamation suit. An employment attorney and a seasoned human resources professional should manage the mechanics of the employee's exit and any existing issues like possible violations of restrictive covenants.

For the departing executive, the lesson is that the executive must remind the employer that the executive does not expect and will not tolerate the employer making *untrue* disparaging statements. Sometimes a warning communication from the executive's attorney is needed.

Waivers and Releases

The separation agreement may be also called a settlement agreement, a release agreement, or a severance agreement. One provision that is usually in separation agreements is a waiver and release provision that requires one or both parties to agree not to bring claims or lawsuits against the other.

Waiver and Release Are Pretty Standard

Employers almost always have a waiver and release provision that runs in their favor in separation agreements. The employer's obtaining a waiver and release from the departing employee is usually the major incentive for the employer to agree to give the employee a severance payment.

Reciprocity

The departing executive should also insist upon having a provision that waives and releases the employer's claims and causes of actions against the executive. The waiver and release provisions should be reciprocal to be fair. The waiver and release should cover any existing or potential and known and unknown claims or causes of action.

Kinds of Claims Covered

The release provision in favor of the employer is ordinarily quite lengthy and includes every possible claim or cause of action that the employee could bring or initiate against the employer. The employer's waiver and release provision covers violations concerning employment contracts, employee handbooks, the Fair Labor Standards Act, the Americans with Disabilities Act, the Employee Retirement Income Security Act, the Family Medical Leave Act, the Age Discrimination in Employment Act, state minimum wage acts, state wage payment and collection acts, and so forth.

Kinds of Persons and Entities Covered

The release of the employer will also specifically discharge every entity and everybody associated with employer, such as its subsidiaries, affiliates, directors, officers, administrators, employees, agents, attorneys, successors, assigns, and each person acting in the name of or on behalf of employer.

Global Application

The waiver and release provision can be made absolute and comprehensive as to private party causes of action, as opposed to any government-initiated actions. Typical language used to ensure comprehensive application of the release can be something like the following:

> It is the intention of the parties not to limit this release to claims arising out of or in the scope of Employee's employment by Employer and to make this release as broad and as general as the law permits.

Non-Waivable Claims and Carve-Outs

Each party should have a clear understanding of any limitations of, or carve-outs in, the waiver and release. If there are any limitations or carve-outs, they should not be so vague and subjective that the complaining party can arbitrarily and capriciously file a claim or lawsuit, thus defeating the purpose of the waiver and release. There is something to be said for achieving finality of non-liability for the parties so that each of them can move on. However, if one party, the employer for example, feels strongly that certain possible claims cannot be waived because of unanticipated bad publicity, liability to third parties or regulatory scrutiny or strong moral imperatives, then that party should carve out egregious claims such as malfeasance. Some claims cannot be legally waived.

Typical language excluding non-waivable claims would be something like this:

> Excluded from this waiver and release is any claim or right which cannot be waived by law, including all claims arising after the date of this Agreement and Employee's worker's compensation claim, the right to file a charge with or participate in an investigation conducted by an administrative agency, and the right to enforce this Agreement.

So many waiver and release provisions have become boilerplate that many attorneys and clients do not scrutinize them as they should. Each separation agreement may have different circumstances and its waiver and release language must be viewed anew and crafted to meet the exigencies of the parties' employment relationship.

Covenants Not to Sue

"A covenant not to sue," as the term suggests, is a legal promise not to file a lawsuit. It is usually a companion provision to releases and waivers in a release agreement. Releases and waivers are part and parcel in employment separation/severance agreements. Lawyers drafting separation/severance agreements favor including a covenant not to sue because it can be raised as an affirmative defense in litigation if the party giving the covenant not to sue then decides subsequently to file a lawsuit.

Since the employer's attorney is the person who usually draws up the initial draft of a separation agreement, the covenant not to sue is a provision that an employee reflexively concedes to an employer without much thought. When I represent the employee, I negotiate for the covenant not to sue to be mutual — what's good for the goose is good for the gander.

If the employer requires peace of mind that the separation agreement will prevent future controversies, then the employee should have the same.

In a separation/severance agreement, a covenant not to sue is subject to certain limitations and exceptions concerning:

1. an employee's ability to file administrative charges with the Equal Opportunity Commission and corresponding state or local agency;

2. an employee's ability to file a lawsuit to challenge whether the employee signed the agreement knowingly and voluntarily for purposes of the Age Discrimination in Employment Act;

3. an employee's ability to be a witness in a class action suit against the employer; and

4. an employee's ability to waive a right when the waiver is prohibited by law.

FINAL POINTS:

Although releases and covenants not to sue are usually set out together in a separation/release agreement, there is a subtle difference between them. A release gives up or relinquishes a right to enforce a right or a claim that could have been enforced, while a covenant not to sue is an agreement not to assert a right to bring a cause of action in court. Put another way, a release extinguishes a right and a covenant not to sue does not allow a right to proceed to litigation. A permanent or perpetual covenant not to sue, as opposed to a set time limit not to sue, has the same effect as a release or discharge.

This may be too much information for the typical executive to know or care about. The important thing to remember is to make reciprocal both releases and covenants not to sue.

Prevailing Party's Litigation Expenses

A common provision in employment agreements, separation agreements, or stand-alone agreements containing restrictive covenants (*e.g.* non-competition and non-solicitation) is a "prevailing-party" provision. This kind of provision grants the prevailing party in any litigation concerning an agreement the right to be reimbursed for its, his, or her legal fees and costs.

A typical prevailing-party provision will read like the following:

> If litigation arises under this Agreement between the Company and the Executive, the prevailing party in such litigation shall be entitled to recover its or his reasonable attorneys' fees, court costs, and out-of-pocket litigation expenses from the non-prevailing party.

The prevailing-party provision serves as a disincentive for an individual employee to assert his legal rights or to take a risk of violating an agreement. From the outset, the employer ordinarily would have more financial resources to litigate, and this added provision of saddling the non-prevailing party with all the litigation costs has a chilling effect on the employee's seeking vindication of his rights. From the employer's standpoint, this is precisely the sobering reminder that an employer wants to send to its ex-employees who may choose to test the validity of the employer's restrictive covenants, especially non-compete clauses.

In any event, the prevailing-party provision is one that must not be overlooked by either the employee or the employer.

Dodd-Frank Act and Severance Payments

The Dodd-Frank Wall Street Reform and Consumer Protection Act ("Dodd-Frank") is legislation that responded to the financial meltdown that occurred toward the end of the last decade and contains the greatest federal legislative financial reforms since the Great Depression of the 1930s.

Among other provisions, Dodd-Frank provides shareholders with an advisory vote on all severance compensation paid to named executive officers (principal executive officer, principal financial officer, and three other of the most highly compensated executive officers) upon an acquisition, merger, or consolidation, or upon a proposed sale or disposition of all or substantially all the assets of a public company. In other words, this is Dodd-Frank's provision for shareholder approval of so-called "Golden Parachute" compensation. Dodd-Frank specifically requires the vote on this shareholders' resolution to approve Golden-Parachute compensation to be separate from any shareholder vote to approve an acquisition, merger, consolidation, or similar act.

As a result of Dodd-Frank, corporate board compensation committees must be much more rigorous in setting and justifying the compensation paid to the top executives of their respective companies.

Claw-Backs

A claw-back provision, under certain conditions, permits a company to demand repayment of compensation previously paid to its executives. Those conditions usually involve compensation paid to executives based on performance measures or factual circumstances that later turn out to be inaccurate, false, or fraudulent. It can be based on statute or by contract.

Did you know that the Chairman and CEO of United Health Group, Inc. had to give back $468 million in cash bonuses, sold stock, and remaining stock options? Because of the purported misconduct of options backdating, his compensation was "clawed back" from him by the powerful paw of the U.S. Securities and Exchange Commission in a 2007 settlement agreement. This occurred even before the ongoing controversy over perceived excessive executive compensation in our not-so-long-ago times of near economic global implosion.

What the Company Giveth, it Taketh Away

Use of claw-back provisions in executive compensation plans and employment agreements is increasing. As noted above, a claw-back provision, under certain conditions, permits a company to demand repayment of compensation previously paid to executives. Those conditions usually involve compensation paid to executives based on performance measures or factual circumstances that turn out to be inaccurate, false, or fraudulent. An example is where earnings are mis-stated and those earnings were used as a justification, validation, or trigger for a performance bonus or other compensation.

By statute and contract, our free market economies attempt to regulate or bind executives to uphold and adhere to legal and moral conduct.

Can we legislate ethics or contract for morality? The Ten Commandments is a combination of law and covenants to do the right thing. We also have claw-back laws on the books like the Sarbanes–Oxley Act of 2002 and the U.S. Bankruptcy Code, and in the case of not-for-profits, state statutes and common law.

A person's reputation takes years to build and only a minute to be destroyed by some real or perceived illegal or immoral act. Executives must be vigilant about their ethics and business choices.

The public — whether residents of Main Street America, the self-described 99 per centers, or good corporate governance types — really is fed up with reckless, risky corporate financial behavior and outsized compensation packages that bear little relation to performance by the executives receiving them. Greed is not good. For executives, ethical behavior is always the right thing to do personally, organizationally, and globally.

Claw-back mechanisms are necessary to do justice and to reassure the public that fairness, honesty, and proportionality will be promoted and protected when there are uncertain, unstable economic times and there is much economic hardship. Such conditions make ripe the seeds of class warfare that always lie under the surface of a capitalist economy.

I love capitalism and there is no better system than capitalism; however, it cannot be unbridled and must be tempered with appropriate controls like statutory and contractual claw-back provisions.

TARP

TARP is an acronym for Troubled Asset Relief Program, our U.S. government financial bailout for companies that were deemed too big to fail.

During the Great Recession of 2009, corporate reform activists as well as such 800-pound gorillas like TARP Pay Czar Kenneth Feinberg, the U.S. Treasury Department's special master, clamored for the utilization of claw-back provisions as a means of protecting shareholders and taxpayers from reckless, dishonest, or avaricious executives whose actions could destroy a company or wreck an economy — think Enron and Lehman Brothers. Of course, a reckless, dishonest, or avaricious executive is all in the eye of the beholder — it may or may not be true. Fortunately for the executives of companies who had received TARP funds, Feinberg was hesitant to invoke his claw-back powers.

Both boards of directors and CEOs must get used to the idea of claw-back provisions, as their application and implementation may be becoming the norm a lot quicker than they anticipate.

Claw-Back: SEC Style

The Securities Exchange Commission (SEC) has the power to claw back compensation paid to executives by their companies under certain circumstances. The statutory basis of the claw-back power against perceived wayward executives is Section 304 of the Sarbanes-Oxley Act of 2002 (SOX). We noted above that SOX made CEOs and CFOs of companies that are subject to any securities laws' financial reporting requirements, liable for repayment of compensation or profits received based on financial mis-statements that necessitated an accounting restatement.

Expanding Use of Claw-Back

On August 30, 2011, the SEC announced its settlement with the former CFO of Beazer Homes USA, an Atlanta-based homebuilding company. Although the SEC did not personally charge the CFO with misconduct, the SEC forced him to reimburse his former company over $1.4 million in compensation that he received arising from fraudulent financial statements. SEC Atlanta Regional Director Rhea Kemble Dignam commented, "O'Leary received substantial incentive compensation and stock sale profits while [his company] was misleading investors and fraudulently overstating its income."

Absence of Charge Not Enough

The CFO was vulnerable to the claw-back even though it was the company's chief accounting officer who was actually charged with perpetrating the fraudulent overstatement of the company's income. The SEC stated in its press release:

> Section 304 requires reimbursement by some senior corporate executives of certain compensation and stock sale profits received while their companies were in material non-compliance with financial reporting requirements due to misconduct...[including] an individual who has not been personally charged with underlying misconduct or alleged to have otherwise violated the federal securities laws.

Trust But Verify

What is the lesson to be learned from this case? CEOs and CFOs must be ever vigilant in ensuring that the financial statements of their companies are not misleading or fraudulently prepared by employees. They must treat their accounting employees the way President Ronald Reagan treated the Russians in his nuclear missiles treaty: "Trust but verify." Even when they may not be personally charged with wrongdoing, the SEC may still hold them personally responsible and require them to disgorge their compensation. Who said life was fair?

PARTING WORD:

Ethical behavior and utmost integrity are the best ways to make the executive's compensation "claw-proof."

On the Other Hand

In August 2003, the NYSE board of directors approved a total of $187.5 million in compensation to Chairman and CEO Richard A. Grasso. As bits and pieces of the compensation became public, Grasso and the NYSE became embroiled in a firestorm that eventually led to Grasso's forced resignation. The New York Attorney General at the time, the ever-enterprising and now disgraced Eliot Spitzer, filed a lawsuit seeking the return of $100 million out of the $139 million in compensation that had been paid to Grasso by the NYSE. Grasso fought back, both in the court and in the media. He prevailed! He was saving his money and his reputation at the same time. Both are important. At different points in a person's life, money may be more important to the person than reputation, and vice versa.

This goes to show that each case must be evaluated on its own merits. Rolling over and being passive in a claw-back scenario may not be justified. For other executives, when they have done wrong, the honorable thing to do is to take their lumps and show remorse. In any event, the lessons here are that an executive should consider at the outset whether the claw-back was deserved, and, if not, whether to hire public relations counsel to complement the legal counsel already retained. As Grasso proved, the retention of vigorous public relations and legal counsel is money well spent.

Also, the idea that a contract should be honored and upheld, no matter how excessive the compensation may appear to third parties, is fundamental to the rule of law and the protection of property — without which we cannot have an effectively functioning market economy or democracy. If third parties find fault with a compensation package, they need look no further than the compensation committee of the board of directors. Whether a board's compensation committee has properly carried out its duties, responsibilities, and obligations is a different matter to consider.

Non-Circumvention Agreements

"Trust in God does not supersede the employment of prudent means on our part. To expect God's protection while we do nothing is not to honor but to tempt providence."

~Pasquier Quesnel

Executives and professionals who have left their organizations for one reason or another and are bursting with great ideas for business opportunities must learn how to protect those business opportunities. We have all heard stories from people who lament that "my business idea was stolen from me" or "this person I trusted cut me out of the very deal that I conceived." A well-drafted non-circumvention document could have protected them from such shenanigans. A non-circumvention provision or agreement is designed to prevent a party from taking an opportunity or idea brought to this first party by a second party and then doing an end run around the second party to a third party. Typically, the second party expected to engage in or execute some kind of commercial transaction with the first party, in relation to some third party.

The non-circumvention agreement can be mutual, so neither party can go around the other using the information obtained from one another. The third party could be a prospective seller, customer, client, vendor, supplier, investor, inventor, and so on. As the opportunity or idea is usually considered proprietary and confidential, the non-circumvention agreement is often used in conjunction with a non-disclosure/confidentiality provision. Sometimes, for good measure, companion non-competition, non-solicitation, and no-grant-of-license provisions may be added.

What does a scenario for non-circumvention look like? One of my clients was negotiating with an investor to fund an acquisition of unique assets that had tremendous upside value and the client inked an agreement that prevented the investor from directly acquiring the assets from the seller without involvement of my client. A confidentiality provision was also included in the agreement.

What does a non-circumvention provision look like? Here are two examples:

Example 1

> NON-CIRCUMVENTION. The Receiving Party and its officers, employees, and directors will not make any effort to circumvent terms of this Agreement in an attempt to gain the benefits or considerations granted to it under this Agreement by taking any of the following actions: The Receiving Party will not in any way use, sell, transfer, develop, market, finance, or invest in directly or indirectly, through its owners, shareholders, directors, advisors, employees, subsidiaries, agents, or other parties under its direction or control, any product or service that contains or uses the Confidential Information.

Example 2

> NON-CIRCUMVENTION. The Receiving Party agrees
> that it shall not, either directly or through any third
> party, enter into any contract, joint venture, partner-
> ship, or business arrangement, or otherwise conduct
> any business whatsoever with any person, regarding
> the Transaction without the written consent of the
> Disclosing Party.

The upshot in your business dealings is to create trust but construct protection. A non-circumvention agreement is a building block of protection.

Unfortunately, the misappropriation of business opportunities by unethical parties happens too often. In order to successfully do business, you must have a trust quotient. So the watchwords are "trust, but protect."

PART 2

COMPENSATION AND FINANCIAL SENSE

CHAPTER THREE

COMPENSATION: THE BREAD AND BUTTER

Dodd-Frank: Say on Pay

Noteworthy for executives of public companies are Dodd-Frank's statutory provisions concerning shareholders' approval of executive compensation.

At least once every three years, Dodd-Frank (The Dodd–Frank Wall Street Reform and Consumer Protection Act) gives shareholders the right to an advisory vote on the compensation of "named executive officers:" the principal executive officer, the principal financial officer, and the three other most highly compensated executive officers. This vote on executive compensation is commonly called "Say on Pay."

At least once every six years, Dodd-Frank also authorizes shareholders to have an advisory vote to determine the frequency of the shareholders' vote on executive compensation of a public company, that is, whether the Say-on-Pay vote should take place every one, two, or three years.

Dodd-Frank does put a spotlight on too-frequent excessive executive compensation at public companies. As a result of the Dodd-Frank legislation, shareholders in public companies exert more influence on executive pay, with increasing emphasis on applying performance metrics to executive compensation. Because of more scrutiny and assertive critics, board of directors' compensation committees are endeavoring to get executive compensation packages just right. A CEO just showing up to work and looking presidential will not impress prudent compensation committees. Any instinctive goodwill and generosity that compensation committee members may have toward a CEO ought to be overridden by their need to protect their own reputations as objective, clear-eyed stewards of the shareholders' interests.

Nevertheless, Dodd-Frank does not seem to have dampened the enthusiasm of board of directors' compensation committees to provide generous compensation packages to C-suite executives. Many board members are highly compensated executives themselves or friends of the CEO and may be empathetic to the company's top executives' compensation situation. Also, boards may fall prey to a vanity arms race in compensation with peer companies. Finally, boards will usually assert that in order to obtain top executive talent, the companies must provide competitive compensation packages. Unlike their European counterparts, most public company top executives do not have to worry about shareholder revolts or extreme government reactions to extraordinary pay and benefits.

Being a large public company CEO is still a highly coveted, remunerative job.

Vesting

As the saying goes, the only dumb question is the one that isn't asked. Sometimes employees and even sophisticated executives are unsure about the concept of "vesting." The terms "vest" and "vested" are part and parcel of any employee benefits system. Vesting pertains to when an employee's right to a benefit becomes ripe and irrevocable.

For example, "vest" is a term used in describing and accessing employee benefits like retirement payments or grants of stock to employees.

Vesting is the time when specified benefits provided to an employee become certain and complete and are no longer contingent on the employee continuing to work for the employer. When vested, the entitlement to the benefit becomes an absolute right. Unfortunately, this right to a benefit may not mean much if the employer becomes insolvent.

When an executive leaves her employment for any reason, she must scrutinize her benefits materials, employment contract, if any, and her separation agreement, if any, to ascertain to what benefits she is entitled and which benefits have vested. If the benefits materials are dense and confusing, then she should consult her benefits or human resources department to make sure of understanding them. If the employee has engaged an attorney to represent her in her separation, the attorney may also help the employee to evaluate what benefits have or have not vested.

Restricted Stock

When you peruse the financial media and see articles on executives and their compensation, you will often see the term "restricted stock." A widely used form of executive compensation, restricted stock is a grant of stock that vests over time and may or may not be tied to performance measures such as year-end profitability. Restricted stock is frequently tied to length of time working for an employer. A typical grant provides that the shares will vest at the end of a fixed period, say five years from the date of grant, if the executive remains employed by the company.

Restricted stock is usually given as part of a compensation package that includes base salary and other benefits. For example, Executive X is being paid a salary of $800,000 and 180,000 shares of restricted stock valued at $7.5 million as of a certain date. Executive X's stock will vest over several years.

Because the executive usually must be employed for a period of time for the restricted stock to vest, this is a tool for a company to obtain a degree of commitment and longevity from an executive. It can also be used to make whole an executive who has given up benefits and compensation from his old employer to take a job with a new employer.

Although still widely used, stock options have come under criticism for contributing to risky economic or short-term quarterly-profit-maximization behavior. Use of restricted stock seems to be increasing. During the Great Recession of 2009, as a result of the Troubled Asset Relief Program (TARP), "Pay Czar" Kenneth Feinberg, the U.S. Treasury Department's special master, sought to reduce cash payments to the executives of troubled companies and put more emphasis on employees getting more of their compensation in restricted stock linked to their long-term performance. (A history reminder: TARP was our U.S. government financial bailout for companies that were deemed too big to fail.)

My recent experience suggests companies continue to move toward more share-based compensation for their executives. Cash compensation is declining in relative proportion to share-based compensation. Also, the use of restricted stock and restricted stock units is expanding in relation to stock options. An executive's compensation can be a combination of base salary, short-term bonus, stock options vesting at certain points over a few years, and one-time restricted stock units based on performance given on a specified date.

This trend should delight corporate reform activists who have been pushing for appropriate compensation incentives tied to actual performance of executives and to executives' having long-term "skin in the game."

Restricted Stock and IRS Section 83(b) Election

Any Executive who is eligible to receive restricted stock ought to know about the availability of an Internal Revenue Code Section 83(b) election. Not knowing about a Section 83(b) election could result in serious tax consequences for the Executive.

An Executive who is about to receive restricted stock should immediately consult a tax accountant or tax attorney.

Here is a snapshot of Section 83(b) and why it is so important. When a company transfers restricted stock to an Executive in connection with employment, Section 83 provides that the Executive will recognize ordinary income in an amount equal to the excess of the fair market value of the stock as of the date when he or she is no longer subject to a real risk of forfeiture over the amount, if any, paid for the stock.

In the example we are discussing, the Executive's restricted shares are subject to a substantial risk of forfeiture until the five-year vesting period has expired. Thus, under Section 83, the fair market value of the stock at the end of the five-year period will be the amount of taxable income resulting from the grant.

Section 83(b) permits the Executive to make an election, instead, to include the fair market value of the shares in income in the year in which the award was made. If this election is made, the amount of income is determined based on the value of the shares at that time, without regard to the possible forfeiture of the shares.

A major caveat is that the Executive must make the election within 30 days of the receiving the stock. The election form must be sent to the IRS office where the Executive files her personal income tax return. Also, the election form should be sent by certified mail (return receipt requested) to ensure that the Executive has a record that the IRS has received it.

A Section 83(b) election requires careful consideration of the possible benefits and risks. The possible benefit is a saving of income taxes if the value of the shares at the end of the five-year vesting period is higher than their value at the time of grant. The Executive will have shielded from ordinary income tax rates the entire amount of the appreciation during the vesting period. Upon a later sale of the shares, the appreciation that took place during the vesting period will instead be taxed as capital gain.

However, the election also carries significant risks. If the Executive's employment is terminated during the vesting period and a Section 83(b) election was made, the Executive will forfeit the shares but will not be entitled to a deduction for the income taxes paid in the year of the grant. Thus, taxes will have been paid on shares that will never be received.

If the Executive believes the stock will rise in value, believes there is little risk of forfeiture of the stock, and knows that the income that will be reported upon election will be modest, then there may be a strong case for making the Section 83(b) election.

In the context of a restricted stock grant with a five-year vesting period, as in our example, the safest, lowest-risk course is to forgo a Section 83(b) election and recognize the income in the year when the grant vests. The Executive knows in that case that she is paying tax on stock that she owns and that she has avoided the out-of-pocket tax cost that could have resulted had she paid the income tax when she received the stock followed by forfeiture of the very same stock.

Again, the Executive should immediately consult with a tax accountant or tax attorney to analyze her particular employment situation and stock restrictions to determine whether a Section 83(b) election makes sense and to accomplish the election in a timely fashion when the election is warranted.

Investing Well

As I have noted earlier, the equity portion of executive compensation has increased as performance metrics and the length of time spent at a company are utilized to incentivize executives and to justify and rationalize compensation.

Executives must plan early and comprehensively to understand their capital needs for retirement, to determine the extent of their remaining capital, and, then, to invest accordingly.

Concentrated Stock

Concentrated Stock Position Strategies

The first thing for an executive to scrutinize is the amount of concentrated stock (or single stock) holdings. The second thing is to have an appropriate plan for disposition and diversification of the concentrated stock. Failure to do so could affect where the executive ultimately ends up financially. Despite an executive's sentimental feelings about the stock of the company that made his initial fortune, putting all his eggs in one basket could leave him with a lot of cracked eggs.

My expert on this subject is my good friend, **Jason Garcia**, a wealth manager, who graciously allowed me to pick his brain. Here are his insights from my edited interview of him about Net Unrealized Appreciation, 10b5-1 Strategies, Tax Advantage Equity, and Zero Premium Collars.

GARCIA

Risk and Allocation

One of the concerns that Executive Officers have, from a number of different sectors and industries, is their exposure to risk, per the concentration of company stock they accumulate throughout the course of their careers. Due to some rules and regulations, they are limited as to the action they may take with their stock throughout their tenure at the company. As they prepare for retirement, there are also tax and dividend income replacement concerns that they will face as they endeavor to unwind their concentrated positions.

Zero Premium Collars

The Zero Premium Collar is for the individual who has a large quantity of a single stock. The individual does not want to sell the position but he or she would like to minimize the downside risk, without any cash outlay. A zero premium collar is essentially a contract between one individual and a counterparty (typically a broker-dealer) that established both a "floor" and a "ceiling" price on the individual's stock. The contract guarantees that the value of the stock will remain somewhere in between that "floor" and "ceiling" price.

The mechanics of the zero premium collar may be further explained: You would purchase a put option — which gives you the right to sell the stock at a certain "floor" price. This effectively limits the amount of money you can lose, establishing the "floor" price, otherwise known as the "put strike price." You can offset the cost of the put option by selling a call option, which gives the counterparty the right to buy your stock at a "ceiling" price. So, your potential upside gain for your stock would be limited to this "ceiling" price, or "call strike price." Since you buy and sell the put and call contracts simultaneously, there is no premium to be paid.

Zero premium collars generally involve European-style options, which means the counterparty cannot exercise the options before the contract matures. However, you can terminate the contract at your discretion. Your financial advisor can help you determine the most appropriate "floor" and "ceiling" targets, based on the volatility of the stock.

The bottom-line benefits of using a zero premium collar are:

1. You limit your downside risk.

2. You maintain market value appreciation up to a certain level.

3. *You are not required to make an initial cash outlay.*

4. *You retain your voting rights during the contract term.*

5. *Your taxes are deferred until the contract is settled.*

6. *You can borrow against the position.*

Consulting with your financial planner and tax advisor is the best course to determine whether or not a zero-premium collar strategy is best for you.

Net Unrealized Appreciation

Net Unrealized Appreciation or NUA is another useful financial tool. If you participate in a 401(k), ESOP, or other qualified retirement plan that lets you invest in your employer's stock, you need to know about net unrealized appreciation — a simple tax deferral opportunity with an unfortunately complicated name.

When you receive a distribution from your employer's retirement plan, the distribution is generally taxable to you at ordinary income tax rates. A common way of avoiding immediate taxation is to make a tax-free rollover to a traditional IRA. However, when you ultimately receive distributions from the IRA, they'll also be taxed at ordinary income tax rates. But if your distribution includes employer stock (or other employer securities), you may have another option. That is, you may be able to defer paying tax on the portion of your distribution that represents net unrealized appreciation (NUA). You won't be taxed on the NUA until you sell the stock. What's more, the NUA will be taxed at long-term capital gains rates — typically much lower than ordinary income tax rates. This strategy can often result in significant tax savings.

So, the mechanics of NUA operate as follows: A distribution of employer stock consists of two parts: 1) the cost basis (that is, the value of the stock when it was contributed to, or purchased by, your plan), and 2) any increase in value over the cost basis until the date the stock is distributed to you. This increase in value over basis, fixed at the time the stock is distributed in-kind to you, is the NUA.

For example, assume you retire and receive a distribution of employer stock worth $500,000 from your 401(k) plan, and that the cost basis in the stock is $50,000. The $450,000 gain is NUA. How does the NUA tax strategy work?

At the time you receive a lump-sum distribution that includes employer stock, you'll pay ordinary income tax only on the cost basis in the employer securities. You won't pay any tax on the NUA until you sell the securities. At that time the NUA is taxed at long-term capital gain rates, no matter how long you've held the securities outside of the plan (even if only for a single day). Any appreciation at the time of sale in excess of your NUA is taxed as either short-term or long-term capital gain, depending on how long you've held the stock outside the plan.

At the end of the day, the following are the advantages of electing NUA:

1. *Your distribution of NUA will be taxed at long-term capital gains rates, rather than ordinary income tax rates.*

2. *Your distribution won't be subject to the required minimum distribution rules that would apply if you rolled the distribution over to an IRA. You need never sell the stock if you don't want to.*

3. *The NUA portion of your distribution will never be subject to the 10% early distribution penalty tax.*

Consulting with your financial planner and tax advisor is the best course to determine whether or not NUA is best for you.

10b5-1 Strategy

Determining the best time to purchase and sell stock to take full advantage of the market is never simple. Company blackout periods and insider trading restrictions can make it even more difficult for corporate executives to manage their liquidity and find an opportunity to increase (or reduce) their single-stock exposure.

By way of background, we know that insiders/executives have historically experienced difficulty in trading their company stocks due to blackout periods established by their own companies. In October 2000, the SEC created 10b5-1, which dramatically expanded the time period during which such trading could occur. As long as an insider/executive established a trading plan while not in possession of material inside information, future trading can occur at any time, even during blackout periods.

A 10b5-1 trading plan allows the purchase and sale of stock at a predetermined time and price. Once established, the plan remains in effect even during times when you are aware of material, nonpublic information that might have influenced your trading decision. It's important to note that a properly executed 10b5-1 trading plan becomes a documented affirmative defense against allegations of insider trading.

It's also important to note that company executives remain subject to legal compliance. So, establishing a 10b5-1 plan does not relieve them from compliance with their company's insider trading policies. It is recommended that any corporate executive considering this trading plan engage legal counsel like you and your law firm, G. A. — as well as investment professionals experienced in 10b5-1 trading plans. Ultimately, the trading plan should also be approved by the executive's company counsel.

Tax Advantaged Equity

We all know that taxes can significantly reduce investor returns. Indeed, taxes can represent the single largest cost of investing for taxable investors. Tax considerations are especially important for investors who:

1. *have experienced or are about to experience the sale of a business;*

2. *have sold or are about to sell a significant concentration of company stock; or*

3. *are tax-sensitive.*

Fortunately, portfolios can be managed effectively to preserve wealth through a tax advantaged equity (TAE) strategy.

The mechanics of a TAE operate as follows: It combines an equity benchmark exposure with a proprietary active tax management process. Within a separately managed account, we approximate the risk and return characteristics of a particular benchmark (e.g., S&P 500). We then proactively harvest losses in a manner customized to your individual tax and investment goals. This approach can help protect the returns obtained through a traditional active manager by:

1. *realizing losses in specific securities that have decreased in value; and*

2. *limiting the turnover in securities that have increased in value.*

In addition to managing risk to meet client specifications, we also consider the impact of security sales and resulting tax implications that may affect the portfolio. This tax-efficient solution can be used alone, or in combination with a core investing approach or other satellite strategies, such as single-stock exposure management; active fixed income; and hedge fund, private equity, or manager-of-managers programs.

At the end of the day, employing an effective TAE strategy can yield the following benefits:

1. *Provide pre-tax returns similar to a benchmark (minimizing tracking error).*

2. *Deliver after-tax, value-added returns through active management (particularly loss harvesting).*

3. *Provide customized management in a separate account vehicle.*

4. *Reflect specific stock or sector limits based on social screens or other concentrated positions.*

Jason Garcia gives the executive much to think about and to carefully consider in maximizing the value of and return on his or her stock holdings.

Making the Most of Your Compensation

How do you manage cash and share-based compensation? You must analyze the effect of inflation, taxes, and spending, and utilize multiple investment vehicles. In my discussions with my friends at Bernstein Global Wealth Management, they have run simulated observations resulting in distributions of 10,000 outcomes and probability distributions, giving us an idea of what can happen with an executive's allocation of investments of cash, restricted stock, and stock options. Essentially, a risk/reward analysis can be done for cash, restricted stock, and a 10-year stock option. Probable results at the end of 10 years after taxes and inflation, assuming cash was re-invested in diversified global stocks and the vesting assumptions were the same for the cash, restricted stock, and stock options:

- Cash grants (invested in global stocks) generated the highest median return and provided the best return in poor market conditions, but had limited upside.

- Restricted stock grants provided wider return, had lower downside and greater upside, but much lower return than the cash grant.

- Stock option grants had tremendous upside, but the downside was also high, especially with worthless expired options; thus they have the lowest median result of the three grants.

Assuming you have maximized your pre-tax contributions to your retirement plans, then another approach is to use a deferred annuity, as the tax deferred treatment of any accumulation can help manage the impact of taxes.

Although permanent whole life insurance is purchased primarily for the death benefit, over time, it accrues cash values which may generally be protected from creditors, as are most retirement accounts, depending upon the state in which you reside.

When all is said and done, it is critical to use a sophisticated financial advisory firm in managing your finances.

Unit Appreciation Rights

Unit Appreciation Rights (for limited liability companies, and known as Stock Appreciation Rights for corporations) are a form of executive compensation tied to the performance of a set amount of units or shares within a set time period. They could include only compensation tied to the amount of increase in the value of the equity, or compensation that comprises both such increase and the original value of the equity.

The compensation may be cash payments or equity equivalent, based on the original full value of a number of units that an executive holds and/or any increase in value (the difference between the price of the units at the time of grant and the price of the units upon exercisability). When an executive exercises her right, a company's Unit Appreciation Rights Plan may allow the company to pay in cash or real common equity of the company, or a combination thereof.

The units granted under Unit Appreciation Rights are not real units of ownership in a company entity, but rather are hypothetical "Phantom Units." The company will grant an executive a number of units, say 3,000, which will have an initial price per Phantom Unit, *e.g.* $30.00. The units will vest after a set period, such as two years after the date of grant, while the executive is still employed. After vesting and before any expiration date, the Unit Appreciation Right becomes exercisable by the executive either in partial amounts or in the full amount depending on the terms and conditions of the company's Unit Appreciation Rights Plan. If not exercised during the executive's lifetime and assuming that an expiration date has not occurred, then any person empowered under the deceased executive's estate ordinarily could exercise the Unit Appreciation Right.

Internal Revenue Code Section 409A

If your employment agreement has deferral of compensation provisions, you may very well see a section or paragraph captioned "Internal Revenue Code Section 409A" or simply "409A." Its official citation is "26 U.S. Code Section 409A — Inclusion in gross income of deferred compensation under nonqualified deferred compensation plans."

This section is too complex and tedious for most layperson executives to understand and figure out. Reading Section 409A of the IRS Code is certainly an instant cure for insomnia.

At the outset, before you execute an employment agreement, retaining an attorney is necessary to interpret Section 409A and apply it to the various scenarios of deferral of compensation to ascertain whether such compensation adheres to Section 409A's deferrals and distributions timing rules.

Failure to comply with the rules concerning deferred compensation has onerous consequences:

1. inclusion of such deferred compensation as gross income for the subject taxable year;

2. payment of the amount of interest on the underpayments; and

3. a penalty amount equal to 20 percent of the deferred compensation, which is required to be included in gross income.

Accordingly, employers often have a Section 409A provision in the employment agreement that allows the employer to adjust payments under the agreement to comply with Section 409A and allows the employer to disclaim any liability to the employee.

A typical provision for 409A can run to lengthy paragraphs and include some language like the following:

> Anything in this Agreement to the contrary notwithstanding, the parties intend that all payments and benefits under this Agreement comply with Section 409A of the Code and the regulations promulgated thereunder and, accordingly, to the maximum extent permitted by law, this Agreement shall be interpreted in a manner in compliance therewith. To the extent that any provision hereof is modified in order to comply with Section 409A, such modification shall be made in good faith and shall, to the maximum extent reasonably possible, maintain the original intent and economic benefit to Employee and Employer of the applicable provision without violating the provisions of Section 409A. Notwithstanding the foregoing, the Employer shall not be required to assume any increased economic burden in connection therewith. Although the Employer intends to administer this Agreement so that it would be exempt from or comply with the requirements of Code Section 409A, the Employer does not represent or warrant that this Agreement will be exempt from, or otherwise comply with, Code Section 409A or any other provision of applicable law. Neither the Employer, its affiliates, nor their respective directors, officers, employees, or advisers shall be liable to the Employee (or any other individual claiming a benefit through the Employee) for any tax, interest, or penalties the Employee may owe as a result of compensation paid out pursuant hereto, and the Employer shall have no obligation to indemnify or otherwise protect the Employee from the obligation to pay taxes pursuant to Code Section 409A.

The point is that your deferred compensation provisions could trigger 409A tax consequences and your employer, through its employment contract with you, is shifting the risk to you as the employee.

Tax Gross-Up

A tax gross-up payment is made by an employer to an employee for any tax liability or penalty an employee incurs because of income, benefits, or perks the employee receives from the employer. This reimbursement by the employer is to make the employee whole concerning the employee's compensation by ensuring the employee nets the full benefit of the compensation intended. Employers have applied tax gross-up payments to compensation and perks ranging from severance payments to club memberships. Corporate reform activists have criticized tax gross-ups and many companies have eliminated them.

PART 3

PROFESSIONAL DEVELOPMENT

CHAPTER FOUR

SOCIAL MEDIA: THE NOT SO BRAVE NEW WORLD

Social Media: Ignore at Your Own Peril

What Is Social Media?

What do you think about LinkedIn? How do you feel about Facebook? What is this Twitter thing? Is Snapchat just for kids? What about Instagram, Pinterest and YouTube? I get asked these questions a lot. I cannot opine on Facebook, Instagram, Pinterest, YouTube or Snapchat because I do not use them. I do use LinkedIn. What do they have in common? Facebook, Twitter, LinkedIn, Instagram, and their ilk are what they call "social media."

The difference between social media and, say, a website or e-mail is that social media is about continuous interactivity and engagement among people who choose to be part of a particular network of individuals. It is basically about information sharing and constant contact and communication through posts. LinkedIn is unabashedly about business and professional networking, and, yes, dignified self-promotion — and ultimately about mutual assistance and leveraging relationships.

LinkedIn Leads the Way for Business Types

My introduction to LinkedIn seems so quaint now. Several years ago, I received a request from a guy with whom I formally worked to "connect" with him on LinkedIn. Not knowing what it was, but not wanting to insult the guy, I agreed to accept his invitation and to register with LinkedIn. In order to register with LinkedIn, I had to give some basic information such as name, current employer, and e-mail. I promptly forgot about it.

Fast forward a year, I am sitting next to Gary at a small dinner party of the Economic Club of Chicago. Gary is a prominent business-to-business marketing guru. At the dinner, Gary was speaking passionately to me and another dinner guest at length about this neat, new phenomenon called LinkedIn that allowed business people and professionals to connect with each other and exchange information with their networks. He said this was the way people would increasingly relate to each other in a commercial setting and that it was like Facebook, but it was geared toward professionals and business people. He further said that the flurry of information from your connections and their connections about their career experience and their current professional and sometimes personal activities was absolutely fascinating and compelling. I thought, *hmmm, if Gary says this is an important feature of future business relationships, I had better pay attention.*

For Many, the Web is the Predominant Way They Make Commercial Decisions

I went on LinkedIn to look at my home page and LinkedIn prompted me to complete my professional profile, to start inviting people to connect with me, and to start making and asking for recommendations/endorsements from my connections. It also encourages you to join affinity groups and to post updates on your activities. It seemed like a lot of work, but I started doing it.

LinkedIn makes it easy to send invitations, as it allows you to import your contacts from Microsoft Outlook or whatever contact system you use. On my LinkedIn home page, my daughter's name popped up as one of many people whom I may know and with whom I may wish to connect. My daughter, Marisol, and I began discussing the utility of LinkedIn and Facebook and she explained to me that she was using them and other Internet vehicles to market her then employer, a high-end custom clothier. She explained to me that her crowd of younger twenty-somethings get most of their news, recommendations, and reviews from the Internet and social media. So Gary and Marisol motivated me to test the waters of LinkedIn, and I am glad they did.

Twelve Things You Should Know About Using Social Media and the Web

Here is what I have learned about social media and the Web:

1. People of the age 45 and under are using the Internet and social media to make a majority of their commercial decisions and, as each year passes, and they grow older, these types of Web users will eventually become the majority of the population. Now we have the Amazon phenomenon and Black Monday Internet shopping sprees. Bricks and mortar retail shops are closing by leaps and bounds.

2. People will "Google" you to research you for their personal or business reasons, so your presence on the Internet had better be a positive image — a strong LinkedIn profile helps greatly.

3. If you do not have a presence on the Internet, you will eventually become invisible, as people will be using fewer other media or forums to hear, see, or learn about you.

4. If you do not have a presence on the Internet, you will begin to be perceived as out of the mainstream and unsophisticated. That sounds harsh, but it is the reality.

5. Your LinkedIn profile and activities updates will educate and remind people, even your family and close friends, of your expertise and skill sets.

6. Employers and executive recruiters are using LinkedIn to search for job candidates; if you are not on LinkedIn, you may not be found.

7. Editors, reporters, and bloggers are using LinkedIn to find subject matter experts or for researching the backgrounds of folks for their articles and stories.

8. Using LinkedIn reinforces and strengthens your off-line relationships with others because you have more information about each other and more reasons to communicate.

9. There are people getting clients, customers, assignments, projects, jobs, and deals through their LinkedIn activities — it works for some folks.

10. There are people *not* getting, clients, customers, assignments, projects, jobs, and deals through their LinkedIn activities — it does *not* work for a lot of other folks.

11. You will be fascinated and surprised about who your connections are "connected to," who is reading your profile, and how many times a week your name comes up in a search.

12. Social Media can become addictive and all-consuming if you are not disciplined about its use — you do not want it to become a huge time-waster.

Social media is clearly not the be-all and end-all of professional visibility and advancement. However, an executive cannot afford not to understand it or not to use it. Rapid change is unforgiving for slow technology adopters in the executive suite. Enough said.

LinkedIn: Closed or Open Networking?

Closed Networker

When I first started using LinkedIn, I was a purist, in that I only invited and accepted invitations from people with whom I had a business or civic relationship. I did not connect to acquaintances. I also tried to keep my LinkedIn network to business and not personal contacts. I did not want to mix the two. I was a closed networker.

If someone I did not know sought to connect to me on LinkedIn, I would either archive the request (now you can simply ignore connection requests) or suggest that the requesting person come by my office to meet me when it was convenient for us both. I wanted to evaluate the person and have a meaningful basis to be in each other's network. I was a little self-conscious and sensitive about the idea of rejecting a requestor and coming off as being exclusive or self-important. As it turned out, meeting every LinkedIn requester was not practical. That idea went nowhere fast.

Open Networker

My thinking later changed for two reasons:

1. I reminded myself that my business and personal worlds were not so compartmentalized and were in many ways seamless, so to limit my LinkedIn network to my business and civic contacts was artificial and counterproductive; and

2. I heard a LinkedIn presenter argue for his open, come one, come all policy.

As a result, I became an open networker and accepted anyone who wanted to connect with me.

I received many requests from people in my various LinkedIn Groups. The requests from some groups like my church men's club, law school, and college were no-brainers. It made sense to connect with fellow parishioners and alumni. Requests from more impersonal groups, like industry groups or city groups, seemed more superficial, but I went with the flow of being an open networker. I also received some random requests from people who shared a mutual acquaintance with me.

Limited, Qualified Networker

My thinking evolved once again and, as I told another student of social networking, I became a limited, qualified networker. I was starting to get requests from people who ranged from pyramid scheme types to people I did not respect to people with whom I would never have any reason to sincerely and meaningfully interface. I felt I was beginning to devalue the capital of my network. Not a good thing from my perspective.

I thought about and decided that developing and expanding one's business network is not a popularity contest. It is not like running for office and seeking as many votes as possible. Also, we all are both inspired and judged by the company we keep. So quality connections do mean something and have real value.

So what is a limited, qualified networker? It is a term I made up. It meant I would be open to networking with folks where I have an existing relationship or where there is a real opportunity to have meaningful interaction in the future. It also meant I would screen and be more selective about whom I will choose to connect with. My intention was not to offend, but to be more effective with the limited time that I have.

The reality is that not all contacts are created equal.

Back to Open Networking

My view has evolved again about being an open networker. Having numerous connections is a net positive in networking even though certain contacts may be more relevant than others. Opportunities and information can come from so many different sources. Let's be honest and practical: Our LinkedIn profiles are billboard resumes. Also, Internet visibility is critical and having a platform from which to distribute one's blog articles or presentations is also important. As a bonus, I do not have to update my contact list every time someone moves or changes jobs. LinkedIn and social media generally are where the commercial, civic, and social action is. There is no barrier to entry and no limits to expression whether it is blogging, podcasting, videoing, photographing or commenting. I see merit in remaining flexible and adaptable in our rapidly changing technological landscape and not remaining static in our views and assumptions.

LinkedIn Is Flexing Its Muscles: Are You Flexing Yours?

The fact that LinkedIn was bought by Microsoft and has over 500 million plus members worldwide says a lot about LinkedIn's impact on social media and its evolving potential.

I have reached my own milestone with LinkedIn, as I have over 2100 connections, a robust number. What does this all mean for my use of LinkedIn?

It is clear that LinkedIn is growing by leaps and bounds and is the dominant game for professional social networking, notwithstanding Facebook. Most LinkedIn members are still in the infant stages of utilizing its full potential.

People are using LinkedIn to post and view updates from their connections. I think more people view updates than post them, so the posters do get a lot of visibility. I know that posting updates does provide opportunities for off-line conversations with my connections. A fellow board member will say, "Oh, I saw the item about your family being on the early morning news show for your children's first day back to school." This comment begins a conversation. The trick is not to become a serial, pesky updater and thus part of the Internet noise that we all are trying to reduce.

I have been able to get people job interviews for advertised positions when I have used my LinkedIn connections at a particular company or organization to facilitate an introduction.

LinkedIn does post jobs in particular fields and has plenty of room to grow. The company states on its website that it "has a diversified business model with revenues coming from hiring solutions, marketing solutions and premium subscriptions." Clearly, it intends to become the go-to source for employment recruiters and job seekers.

The one current drawback to LinkedIn is that many people, if not most, do not check the site frequently, so an update or an e-mail message can get stale. LinkedIn needs to create more incentives to visit its site a couple of times a day rather than a couple of times a week or a month. Recently, LinkedIn has added an article publication feature that should encourage its members to publish blog-like articles. On the home page, people are posting more article links and videos on their updates.

As I have said in earlier commentary on social media, an executive or professional cannot afford *not* to be on LinkedIn, as it is increasingly becoming the dominant venue for people to check out the executive or professional. Again, LinkedIn is a free billboard to let people know who you are, what you have done, and what you can do. Now it should also be about what interesting things you are doing now.

All things being equal: Why wouldn't you be on it? Why wouldn't you file updates? Why wouldn't you accept a connection request?

LinkedIn Photo: Can You Skip It?

A general counsel friend wanted to revise and make more robust his LinkedIn profile and queried me as to whether it was necessary to have a photo. He may have been self-conscious about his looks. Join the club. Aren't we all? He did want his revised profile to be seen by possible recruiters. He also had a question about revealing one's religion on LinkedIn, and that will be discussed later in this chapter.

Mirror, Mirror on the Wall

Many people are self-conscious about their photos and just do not like being photographed. Some do not like the way they look because of age, weight, baldness or whatever. Some do not like the idea of others having photos of them for privacy or security reasons. So having their photo out there on the Internet on LinkedIn makes some people very uncomfortable.

Being Judged

For purposes of using your LinkedIn profile as a resume billboard for a job search or business development, it gets even trickier. Some people do not want to be excluded for consideration for a job or a contract because of race, ethnicity, age, average looks, and so forth. We all know that people can be discriminated against for those reasons (race and ethnicity were not the concerns of my general counsel friend as he is neither a racial nor an ethnic minority). Unfortunately, research has shown physical attractiveness can give a person a leg up in life. Nevertheless, for a job interview or for a business meeting, you will eventually have to meet potential employers or customers in person.

Let It Be

You are who you are, and you should be at ease with yourself even if there are nincompoops who may not be comfortable with your identity, looks, or background.

My personal belief is that if someone wants to discriminate against me because of my age, looks, ethnicity, or whatever, I would not want to work or do business with that person anyway. People are naturally curious as to what a person with whom they may do business looks like. I know that I am. A photo provides more context and makes the profile more interesting. Accordingly, I have no hesitation in putting my photo on LinkedIn.

If I were a woman, I would probably be a bit more circumspect because of security concerns, as there are weird people out there in the world.

BOTTOM LINE:

You can skip a photo on LinkedIn without sacrificing the effectiveness of your profile.

LinkedIn: Is It Okay to Reveal Your Faith-Based Activities?

My general counsel friend, who was updating his LinkedIn profile, asked me whether it was prudent to list his activities related to his Roman Catholic faith. He was concerned about turning off legal recruiters and potential employers by revealing his substantial commitment to his church and faith-based organizations. I kidded him that he was not Jack Kennedy running to become the first Catholic president of the United States. We have come a long way from 1960 in terms of religious prejudice. But he does raise an important point.

Diminishing Religious Discrimination

There were some people who thought Chicago would not elect a Jewish mayor, and that notion seems laughable now. Commentators have noted that Republican presidential candidate Mitt Romney had to overcome an anti-Mormon bias among significant conservative and evangelical elements in his party. Muslim Americans certainly have to contend with stereotypes. We have elected our first African-American U.S. president, so should we be concerned about residual religious bias in the social media market place?

I certainly do not dismiss the fact there remain various degrees of discrimination and bigotry, whether it be based on religious, ethnic, racial, or other factors. Should that fact dictate what we reveal about ourselves in our LinkedIn profiles?

Appropriateness of Religious Information

If your non-business pursuits reflect your substantial commitment to your faith-based activities and you want to share your religious interests publicly, then by all means you should do so. However, if you want to proselytize your religion on your LinkedIn page, then you will likely alienate potential employers or customers. LinkedIn, after all, is about business. If your religion is a big part of your public identity, or if you are a member of the Christian clergy, a rabbi, or an imam, then listing your religious activities certainly makes sense.

Your Story on LinkedIn

For many executives and professionals, their references to religious-related organizations simply round out a picture of their non-work-related, non-profit, and charitable endeavors. For example, I list the fact that I was chair of St. Joseph Seminary at Loyola University of Chicago Board of Advisors and that I am a member of the Queen of All Saints

Basilica Men's Club (including being an assistant Webelos Cub Scout Den Leader at the Basilica.) Although I do not wear it on my sleeve, I am proud to be a Roman Catholic, and revealing that fact tells people something about me — it contributes to my story.

Your LinkedIn profile is a piece of your narrative. Executives and professionals should think carefully about how they craft their narratives.

As I wrote earlier about putting your photo on your LinkedIn profile, if someone wants to discriminate against you because of your age, looks, ethnicity, race, or whatever, you would not want to work or do business with that person anyway. I would add religion to that list.

Use of Common Sense

As it is in everything in life, moderation is the watchword. If your career pertains to faith-based organizations, then a long list of religious-oriented activities would make sense. If you are an executive for a Fortune 500 company and all your listed activities are religious-based, you may limit your potential opportunities within your company as well as with other employers. The more employers perceive your experience to be well-rounded — professional or otherwise — the better.

Politics and LinkedIn

During the 2016 presidential election cycle and afterwards, I saw LinkedIn updates and discussions about whether talking politics or curating politically tinged or themed posts and links and other materials is appropriate on LinkedIn. It is clearly because of the political season and the stridency and controversy surrounding the 2016 presidential election that political matters have spilled over into the business social medium of LinkedIn.

We would expect people to discuss political subjects on Twitter, Facebook, Instagram, and YouTube. However, we would not expect the typical business with a presence on Twitter or Facebook to engage in political discussions. Businesses exist to make money for their owners and managers and employees, and they do that by attracting customers and clients, not repelling them with unfavorable messaging. Professionals want to get hired by a client or recruited by or promoted by an employer, not to turn off the employer or the client. Growing up as a young adult, I was always told that one should avoid talking about politics or religion if one wanted to steer clear of controversy and keep conversations pleasant. Although it was a general statement, I knew that this rule was honored in the breach when it came to discussions with family, friends, and neighbors, and in one's various clubs and affinity groups. What was clear, nonetheless, was that the prohibition on speaking about politics and religion in polite society was to be strictly adhered to in the workplace. This is great advice and a good personal policy to have.

We have seen businesses make policy and business decisions to affirm or condemn certain actions that have a political or ideological cast to them. These are sometimes viewed as ethical, moral, justice, or religious values stances. Some corporate boards or business owners choose to undertake a risk of adverse impacts on their business in order to do the "right thing" as they see it.

Should one's LinkedIn page be a forum for one's political views? I was an early adopter of LinkedIn. I use it for my business and professional life and to connect with other business people and professionals. If someone works or has worked for a political party, a political candidate, or an elected official, then that affiliation is relevant information if the person chooses to proffer it. It gives me context and background about that person. Would I be interested in updates, postings, or articles that are political? No. Would I post or send an update with a political theme? No. I do not believe most people join LinkedIn for political content. They join it to present their credentials to the world and to see other members' credentials and to make possible connections.

Political content is a divider on LinkedIn, not a connector. Political statements can easily offend. Displaying political content can cause one to have fewer professional or business opportunities and not even know the opportunities were missed. Personal political content is more suitable to a blog, a Twitter account, and a non-business website and, perhaps, Facebook and Instagram.

Connecting with Work Colleagues on LinkedIn

A partner at a professional services firm queried me as to the utility or desirability of connecting on LinkedIn to people with whom he works. An excellent question. I told him that it was advisable because it is a way of learning more about what your co-workers do. We think we know all the skill sets, expertise, and work experiences of our co-worker across the hall or next door. Assuredly, we do not know the extent of what our colleagues have done and can do. Assuming your colleagues' LinkedIn profiles are sufficiently built out, you will learn things you never knew about them. For example, you might find yourself saying something like, "I did not know Bill spoke Turkish," or "I did not know Sally used to work for IBM," or "I did not know Maritza had a software patent," or "Who knew Abdul was an Eagle Scout?"

Also, when your colleagues post their updates on LinkedIn, you will learn about the new civic, professional, and personal interests with which they are currently involved. This gives you and your colleagues opportunities for discussion and connectedness and helps build a team culture — an imperative for successful organizations.

Finally, seeing each other's connections should promote opportunities to coordinate business or civic development efforts for your firm and to support each other.

LinkedIn and Other Social Media Communications: Violating Non-Solicitation and Non-Compete Covenants

What I find interesting is the intersection of social media and employment contracts. Now we know that one can affect the other.

It cannot be over emphasized that to their detriment, people have gotten far too complacent about social media like Facebook and Twitter. People forget, first, that what is sent into the Internet may never disappear, and, second, that it can be read by millions of individuals as we have seen with Donald Trump's tweets. Unbeknownst to laypersons, their social media communications could possibly be used in a court of law against them or by an employer to dismiss them. A former law partner of mine was fired from his subsequent high-level government job because of unflattering things he said about a public figure on his Facebook page.

The medium of communication does not change the underlying elements of a cause of action and the need to use carve-outs concerning a restrictive covenant.

The medium or means of communication may vary (*e.g.*, telephone or e-mail), but improper communication is improper communication. You can't solicit a customer or former employer if you have signed a valid non-solicitation provision.

If you already have pre-existing relationships with employees, customers, clients, potential customers, and potential clients, then be sure to list those in a carve-out provision before you sign non-solicitation, non-compete, and confidentiality agreements. There may be overlap between your existing contacts and your prospective employer's contacts and you do not want to be precluded from utilizing them post-employment.

We should not be lulled by the false sense of intimacy and instant camaraderie of social media platforms like LinkedIn and Facebook. Our communications, whether on the Internet or face to face, can have unanticipated legal consequences.

Whether or not a LinkedIn update or message communication to one's contacts will constitute a breach of non-solicitation and non-compete provisions will be driven by the facts of the particular case. Bad facts can land a former employee or her new employer in hot water.

It bears repeating that the medium of communication, whether it is telephone, e-mail, mail, fax, or social media, does not change the substance of improper communication that may violate non-solicitation, confidentiality, and non-compete provisions.

As I discussed earlier in this book, employers should notify departing employees that employees' social media may not be used to circumvent any restrictions contained in confidentiality, non-solicitation, and non-compete agreements.

Finally, social media is a still-evolving world of communication that must be approached prudently. You must be conscious of the social, legal, and business impacts of whatever messages and images you are putting on the Internet.

Ten LinkedIn Advice Quick Hits and Observations

1. You should comment on the updates from the members of your network, because it increases your interactivity, visibility, and communication with your network, which is the whole point of establishing a network.

2. You should not forget to provide frequent updates on what you are doing, as it will invite comments and messages from your network, and you and your contacts will discover an opportunity to chat about a mutual interest — again, this is the whole point.

3. On LinkedIn, your updates do not have to be 100% business or professionally related. LinkedIn is not Facebook or Twitter, so you do not want to post a lot of trivial activities or very personal information, but you do want to paint a multi-dimensional, uncontroversial picture of your life and personality beyond strictly business.

4. You can integrate your LinkedIn to your Smartphone so that you have 24-hour access.

5. If you use Microsoft Outlook, you can integrate LinkedIn to your contacts and e-mail. You can do this via the Tools button at the bottom of your LinkedIn homepage.

6. You can find LinkedIn affinity groups that you are truly interested in joining, such as your college, industry, clubs, employer, and this becomes an easy way to stay informed and to connect with people with whom you have something in common. I limit the number, as I feel I have only so much time to consume the information that they generate in terms of discussions, news, and so forth. Other LinkedIn users have a different philosophy and believe that the more groups you join, then the broader and more useful your network becomes. You have to decide what makes sense for you.

7. Although this is stating the obvious, it cannot be stressed enough — triple check your LinkedIn profile to make sure it is correct. Think of all the politicians who had inaccurate, sloppy, exaggerated, wrong, or false information about themselves on their on-line profiles and bios and the resulting grief that they endured.

8. Use your LinkedIn common connections to warm up a cold call — *e.g.,* mention a mutual contact, same college, same church, or similar backgrounds.

9. Some useful applications are:

    a) Uploading presentations on topics that you have spoken or written about

    b) Uploading or linking articles, newsletters, blog posts, videos, and filings

    For example, on the Slide Share Presentation feature, I uploaded a PowerPoint presentation on public construction projects that I created for a seminar given to civil engineers. This simple upload increased my audience on that topic many-fold, and any of my LinkedIn connections can utilize it. When you spend time preparing a presentation or writing an article, you do want people to read it. You will find that the LinkedIn content aggregated on your home page and profile prompts many off-line, in-person conversations with your LinkedIn connections and non-LinkedIn contacts. LinkedIn has become a repository of useful information that can be shared easily.

10. To ask or not to ask, that is the question: you should seek out people you know to connect with them and not wait to be asked, as that is the point of social media — after all, it's not a dating game or popularity contest, but a networking objective. When you are making the connection request, being intentional rather than random about your connections is the idea.

Having said all this about the beauty of LinkedIn, we all should note well that although LinkedIn is a powerful tool and medium, it is no substitute for in-person, face-to-face dialogue with folks. Also, our speaking by telephone or video conferencing is still a useful complement to LinkedIn, other social media, and email.

CHAPTER FIVE

EXECUTIVE SKILLS AND HABITS

Executive Body Language: Do You Have the Right Stuff?

An executive can have a high-achieving resume, an impeccable designer suit, a fresh haircut or new hairdo, and still not get the job, promotion, or the business, because of three simple physical miscues:

1. not smiling
2. having a weak handshake
3. avoiding eye contact

Human beings are animals — social animals — and we take a majority of our information about people from what we see and feel; this goes back to our primitive survival instincts. Fair or not, true or not, accurate or not, a frown can be viewed as threatening; a dish-rag handshake may be interpreted as showing low confidence, being of weak character, or seeming hostile; and an absence of eye contact may connote both insecurity and untrustworthiness (eyes being seen as windows into the soul).

When interacting with people, it pays to be aware of your physical actions. Take inventory. If you fall down in any of these areas, they can be eventually overcome by the executive being sincere, natural, self-aware, and intentional.

Three other image killers to consider:

1. poor posture
2. bad breath
3. unruly nose hair

Poor posture is an obvious one; it suggests the executive is sloppy, too casual, and not confident.

Bad breath is something to which we all can fall victim and sometimes inflict on others. Remember how you feel when you have to engage in an up-close conversation with someone who has foul breath — not a pleasant experience. It is hard to listen closely to someone when your nose is being assaulted, and you will invariably have a negative association about Mr. Stinky Breath.

My wife reminds me never to eat a tuna fish sandwich before talking to someone; I guess that goes for salmon and bagels at a morning meeting or garlic-and-onion–laden foods at lunch or crab cake *hors d'oeuvres* at an evening reception. We cannot forget stale coffee breath, cigarette breath, and alcohol breath too. That is why we have breath mints and gum!

Another pet peeve of my wife (and she is not alone): overgrowth of nose hairs and unruly eyebrows. Your long or overly visible nose hairs waving at everyone are not only distracting to your co-conversationalists, but they simply are not aesthetically pleasing. A bathroom mirror inspection first thing in the morning before that important customer presentation or job interview would be prudent.

Again, fair or not, superficial or not, your poor posture, stinky breath, or conspicuous nose hairs could cost you an opportunity. You can boost and preserve your image by eliminating these image killers.

We cannot emphasize enough the importance of good posture. We have all heard the expression that a person has a "military bearing," which means he stands ramrod straight, chin up, shoulders back, and chest out. The reason the military inculcates erect postures and stances is that they connote authority, discipline, and confidence. Charm schools and etiquette classes also teach correct posture. You usually see models and ballerinas with good posture. It makes you appear taller than you actually are. Even animals like bears and gorillas, when threatened, stand taller and spread their arms to make themselves appear larger and more dominating. Accumulated wisdom through the ages suggests good posture is essential to creating a positive image.

Posture Study

A study by Northwestern University Kellogg School of Management Professor Adam Galinsky and Graduate Student Assistant Li Huang now corroborates this wisdom through their research. Having an open posture of chest high and arms open projects confidence and assertiveness and results in favorable impressions. Great posture also may give a tactical advantage in social intercourse and day-to-day human exchanges. The trick is not to come off as a strutting peacock, but, rather, as a relaxed, comfortable-in-your-own-skin person.

Get Noticed

I do notice men and women who have ramrod straight posture, and I generally have a more favorable impression of them. Obviously, we all know habitually slouching individuals who are also very successful. But in the real world, every bit helps, so why not give yourself an advantage that works? It is such an easy way to stand out and have presence. When my posture is good, I do indeed feel better. It is like wearing a nice suit. More often than not, I have to remind myself about good posture. I am also often reminded when I see poor posture in others, especially my children. When I tell my kids to sit up straight, I can hear my mother's voice.

Executive Writing

We know that it is important that an executive have good speaking skills, whether it is in one-on-one conversation, small group discussions, or large meetings. An executive must know how to make small talk as well as know how to give presentations.

What about writing? Is your writing up to snuff? Whether it is a note, memo, letter, or lengthy report, and, especially a resume, your writing cannot be filled with misspellings, poor punctuation, bad grammar, or inappropriate use of vocabulary. It leaves a poor impression and people will judge you, even if they themselves do not know the difference between "its" and "it's" and use "hysterical" and "hilarious" as synonyms.

An executive need not be a Pulitzer Prize winner, but she must write effectively and in an educated manner, notwithstanding the declining writing standards in texts, tweets, e-mails, and posts. Using the vernacular and improper grammar simply will not do.

Unfortunately, thorough training in writing may be missing in one's high school, college, and graduate school training. The level of writing skills taught is very uneven. Many educated people in the United States find they must teach themselves punctuation and grammar. As there are plenty of good books and articles available on grammar, punctuation, and vocabulary, the paragraphs below will focus only on providing some practical guidelines to keep in mind when writing for business.

There are many elements of effective business and professional writing. Here are a few to start:

- Generally, shorter sentences are better than longer sentences; although, sometimes a complex thought requires a complex sentence, and sometimes a complex sentence is more interesting and effective.

- Shorter paragraphs are better than longer ones.

- The fewer pages you can make a document without omitting critical information, the better.

- An active voice is more powerful than a passive voice; however, sometimes a passive voice just sounds better.

- Simpler words are better than complicated words, *e.g.* "walk" is better than "ambulate."

- The fewer adjectives in your writing, the better, as the facts should be compelling enough for both writer and reader to form conclusions and recommendations.

- You should make sure you know how to use a word, *e.g.*, as the word "irregardless" does not exist, it is considered nonstandard usage and "regardless" is the correct form. Similarly, "Aren't I" sounds elegant, but it is bad grammar: when you convert the contraction to its original full words, it would be "Are I not." "Am I not" is the correct form. In formal writing, it is safer to be a grammatical prig than not — and business writing is formal.

- For long documents, using headings and sub-headings will help guide the reader and break up dense writing.

- It is best to state your proposition or request at the beginning and then follow with arguments and evidence to support your proposition or request.

- If you have compelling data, then use charts and graphs to illustrate your points, as many people are visual learners.

- Triple-check your numerical calculations and data; faulty numbers and simple numerical mistakes will destroy the credibility of your piece; a lack of attention to detail could be seen as a red flag signaling sloppy habits and thinking.

- You should double-check the correct spelling of a person's or organization's name, or place-names, as people are sensitive about their names, affiliations, home towns, and countries; and, again, inattention to detail undermines the reader's confidence in the writer.

- Never totally rely on word processing spell check as it cannot tell the difference between correctly spelled but wrong words like "to" and "too" or "the" and "he" or "be" and "bee" or "of" and "or."

- Whether you are writing a four-sentence letter or a 30-page document, read it with a ruler, line by line, at least three times and have someone else proofread it, too; if you have the time, set the document aside for a few days before doing a final proofread. At least try to sleep on it before sending it out.

- Unless you are a novelist, poet, screenwriter, or playwright, writing in those respective genres, do not use profanity, dialect, crude words, or off-color references in your business or professional writing.

- In formal writing, it is better to write words out fully and not use contractions like "can't" and "don't," because it adds a certain gravity to the communication and shows respect for your audience.

As an executive or professional, you are presumed to be educated, and your bosses, colleagues, clients, customers, and patients will expect that you know how to write well. You do not want to disappoint them.

Oh, and by the way, the only way to improve your writing is by writing. Like anything else, practice makes perfect.

Presenting and Public Speaking

"Speak but little and well if you would be esteemed a man of merit."

~Richard C. Trench

White House Conference

During Obama's presidency, I was at the White House for a conference on education policy. Those who attended the conference were alumni or members of the board of Leadership Greater Chicago Fellowship Program. Several of its alumni populated the Obama administration such as First Lady Michelle Obama, Education Secretary Arne Duncan and Council of Economic Advisors Chairman Austan Goolsbee.

The Obama administration viewed education, innovation, and infrastructure as imperative for America's economic growth and competitiveness. The purpose of the conference was to obtain input from and bounce ideas off of thought leaders in order to make the case for fundamental changes in American education policy. The administration wanted to push for a major expansion of instruction in science, technology, engineering, and math (STEM) in primary and secondary education. During the Obama years, STEM became popularized. Another long-term push was to make the U.S. # 1 in the number of yearly college graduates.

Making a Presentation

Whatever your politics may be, the one thing you can be sure of is that President Obama had very smart, talented, and articulate people working for him. Ten members of his administration, ranging from a cabinet secretary to an economist, presented to us and took our many questions and listened to our many comments and suggestions.

To a person, the Obama staffers were exceedingly articulate. None used a prepared text. Also, none came off as arrogant, conceited, smug, or egotistical. They were persuasive and impressive — not an easy thing to accomplish with this particular audience of recognized leaders.

Executives Must Speak Well

Like the Obama officials, private sector executives should be good presenters. They need not be exceptional presenters, but they must express themselves well. The trick is achieving consistency in quality. An executive must minimize his off-days and try to maintain a minimum standard of effective communication. Not every executive can be a soaring orator or an entertaining speaker. However, an executive can learn to speak knowledgeably and get her ideas across.

An executive can limit his opportunities if he is a poor, ineffectual speaker. Obviously not all successful politicians or captains of industry have been outstanding speakers. But those persons who have mastered an acceptable quality of public speaking have greater chances of success than those who do not.

They say more people fear public speaking than fear death. Even accomplished speakers can get butterflies and their knees can buckle.

Keep It Simple

Any hard-working person can learn effective public speaking. You can always join Toastmasters International, a club that serves as a public-speaking boot camp. I have done Toastmasters, as have my children, and it is a program that works. I am no expert on public speaking and the quality of my own speaking is not as consistent as I would like it to be. It is hard to hit a home run every time you give a speech or a presentation. You do want to get to the level where you will be assured of at least getting on first base. From studying others and from my own experience, I do believe there are certain maxims and tips that are helpful in trying to achieve consistent mastery of public speaking. It helps to:

- Keep your topic simple — no more than three ideas.

- Focus on what exactly is the idea or ideas you are trying to convey.

- Know your subject well.

- Keep your language simple — active voice, few adjectives, and short sentences (similar to effective non-fiction writing).

- Prepare and practice your speech so you get familiar with the cadence, rhythm, pronunciation, and word emphasis.

- Take deep meditation-type breaths leading up to your speech — the breathing does help calm the mind.

- Present often. The more you present, the better you will get, so force yourself to do as many as you can and do not turn down an opportunity to speak, whether or not it is a significant one. Doing speeches as often as you can builds speaking and presentation muscles and skill.

- Try to make your presentation interactive with your audience (if the situation lends itself to this), for instance asking the audience questions or joking with an audience member; it can make the presentation more interesting.

- When appropriate, smile.

We all know of famous and not-so-famous people who have overcome stuttering, stammering, and stage fright to become effective speakers. So can all of us. We cannot all be outstanding speakers, but we all can be decent ones.

Again, public speaking, like any endeavor does improve with focused effort, practice, and study. If you commit to it, you will achieve it.

ONE LAST OBSERVATION:

Try to speak without notes, as that is the most powerful way of public speaking.

Leading by Reading

A companion habit to good writing and speaking is to read a lot. It may sound trite but it is generally true that "leaders are readers." That is not to say that an uneducated person cannot be a leader in his or her own way; nevertheless, reading has its advantages. We have learned that Bill Gates, Oprah Winfrey, Warren Buffett, Elon Musk, Steve Jobs, and Mark Zuckerberg, among many other successful business people, are/were avid readers. Presidents John Adams and Thomas Jefferson read books as far into old age as they physically could and prized their personal libraries. Benjamin Franklin valued books so much that he created the first lending library in America, and we know what a wise and accomplished man he was.

More recent presidents, like Jimmy Carter, William Jefferson Clinton and Barack Obama, are known to like to pick up a book. Whatever your politics may be, well-read leaders are likely to sound erudite, do they not? Their knowledge enables them to sound more persuasive and sound more credible, does it not? An effective executive seeks to become well-read by reading often and reading a variety of genres.

Comparable to reading, but not as much as a deep-seated learning and not, I believe, as satisfying, would be listening to audio books and podcasts and watching substantive videos. When reading, you have time to ponder, contemplate, linger over and ultimately process the content. Your listening to audio or watching videos constitutes a more passive brain activity than the act of reading. It is, of course, better than no learning activity.

The most cerebral people I know, voraciously read books and periodicals. They are well versed on many topics and subjects and are able to connect them, contrast them, compare them, analogize them, extrapolate from them and meaningfully unpack them.

The act of reading or listening to books is the intention and commitment to learn new things and to be in a continuously learning mode — kind of like a continuing liberal arts education. Especially now, the intention-and-commitment-to-learn mode has become imperative given that the rate of expansion of knowledge and innovation seems to double whether in hours, weeks, months or years depending on the field.

My base technology knowledge as a 16-year-old was rather primitive and quaint compared to my 16-year-old son who knows how to put together a computer from off-the-shelf components and to program a robot. He reads articles and blogs on the internet and watches YouTube videos when he wants to learn how to do something. That is useful learning. However, he and my teenage daughter and most other teenagers that I know do not read enough books, let alone wide and deep reading of books. I fear their writing and critical thinking skills and broad-base knowledge could suffer. My base general knowledge as a teenager was far greater than theirs is. I attribute this gap to the fact that I had read many more books by their ages.

By reading, you learn how to write better by seeing word usage, different vocabulary, grammar, punctuation and syntax and hearing in the mind's ear the writer's voice. As I alluded earlier about being well versed, by reading you also know more about different topics to inform your professional or social conversations with others. It can make your conversations more interesting. Moreover, by reading you bring to bear more knowledge to understand and solve problems and ask the right questions in your work whether it be professional or volunteer work. When you face industry disruption, or must be a change agent, or you need to reinvent your business or yourself, your store of knowledge from reading will come in handy!

For those readers for whom reading does not come readily because of lack of habit or interest, or busyness, the trick is to approach it like starting any new program (like physical exercise or learning a new language): begin lightly with 15 minutes a day and incrementally work your way up to a robust hour. You may just remember or find out what you have been missing all these years: the joys of reading. You will grow smarter and stay cognitively sharper longer. Book smarts does not always translate into business smarts, but more acquired knowledge can only be helpful to your development. Oh, and by the way, if you have trouble falling asleep at night, start reading a book; it is quicker and healthier than a sleeping pill.

Potty Mouth in the Workplace

"The foolish and wicked practice of profane cursing and swearing is a vice so mean and low, that every person of sense and character detests and despises it."

~George Washington

Does boorish behavior matter? As part of our daily work routine, we all experience instances where co-workers, bosses, clients, customers, and vendors use profanity, recount indelicate stories, tell off-color jokes, or over-share personal information. It seems that decorum and verbal restraint are neither required nor in vogue anymore. Verbal boundaries have all but disappeared.

Does anybody else miss the polite conversation in the work world that used to be the norm? I am not a prude and have myself used profanity on occasion in work-related situations. I would like to think that the few times I use profanity, it is to emphasize a point or to provide colorful context to a story or an experience. Maybe my perceived degree of use is a distinction without a difference and I am rationalizing my own verbal indiscretions, no matter how limited they may be.

I know that I am turned off by excessive use of profanity and by habitual tellers of dirty or ethnic jokes. I also get uncomfortable when a work-related person over-shares personal information or unusual circumstances, when it is clearly not appropriate to the circumstance of the conversation or the relationship. The initial entertainment value of an over-sharing story begins to lose its appeal pretty quickly, especially from repeat offenders. What may have seemed funny or salacious can then make us cringe.

The repugnancy of indiscriminate and unrelenting use of profanity came into sharp relief to me and other adult leaders when members of my son's Boy Scout troop degenerated into persistent crude remarks on long camping trips. Obviously, many of these teenage boys thought it was cool and clever to curse. The adult leaders thought "not," as it was not Boy-Scout–like behavior, and to permit the boys to develop this habit was doing them a disservice. So we called a meeting with the boys to have a serious talk and straighten them out. Of course, it reminded the adult leaders that "Do as I say, and not as I do" does not play well with kids; so we, ourselves, had to be consistent about our own use of coarse, colorful language no matter what the context — work, home, or out and about.

Despite the increasing coarseness of our popular culture, I think there is something to be said for etiquette — it makes people more comfortable and it reduces the likelihood of offending people. I think that executives and professionals who use little or no profanity, who do not over-share, and who resist off-color humor set themselves apart in a positive way. Crude behavior does have consequences.

Executive Job Interview Readiness

Job interviews are fundamental to professional advancement. Every executive has had a few times, if not many times, when the she did not get the offer. The executive may feel that the she "blew" the interview. The executive may be thinking: Was I too nervous? Was I too rambling in my responses? Did I not ask the right questions? Was my body language off-putting? Was my voice too squeaky?

The executive will analyze the perceived failed interview a thousand different ways. What is very frustrating is that many executives extensively prepare for interviews by researching the company and its people, anticipating the likely kinds of questions, and practicing scripted answers. They were prepared, or so they thought.

What most executives do not know about or consider is an interview coach. Even at the pinnacle of their talents, world class athletes hire coaches to improve their skills. Why would you not get help on how to nail a job interview?

Corinne Vargas is just such a person who can help you up your interview game. She is the founder of CVC Consulting, a firm that offers, among other services, coaching for professional and business interviews. I interviewed this job-interview maven for my blog and the following pearls of wisdom are gleaned from my edited interview of her.

Vargas

Making an Investment in Coaching to Make It to the Next Round

In my experience, the investment is often not the barrier to hiring a coach. Instead, I have found many executives do not consider interview coaching and support for two reasons:

1. *they are eager to start the process of finding a new position and feel they want to tackle it as quickly as possible, which often means alone; or*

2. *they do not know coaching is available for tailored situations.*

Unfortunately, many clients find coaches only after attempting to tackle the process on their own, when they are in various states of rejection, frustration, and desperation.

However, post-coaching, clients often express the lessened anxiety and frustration they felt during the process compared to going it alone. They explain having a coach "on their side" to help them through various steps in the process proved invaluable. Skilled coaches can help clients though different steps or aspects of the process, including interview question preparation, nervous and anxious manifestations, content presentation, transition story framing, and storytelling in the interview context. Coached clients frequently state feeling more control over the process and a higher level of confidence and preparedness, ultimately bolstering a better representation of their personal brand and better outcomes.

My advice to an executive in transition or looking to transition, is that it is worth the time to at least explore having a coach, as it can save time and frustration, and help you achieve your goals with more confidence, focus, and many-times-faster speed. If an executive decides to explore this option, they should look for an interview coach who provides focused, tailored, coaching sessions offering perspective and actionable feedback.

The Process of Interviewing — Coaching

I often start with an informal call with a client to decide if the relationship will be the right fit for the client and their needs. If the fit is right, the initial meeting can be held in multiple modalities, but I prefer in person or via web conference, as this allows me to not only hear the client but see how they carry themselves as well.

The first meeting is focused on relationship-building and learning about my client. It usually consists of an open, free-flowing conversation. I try to gain insight into why the client has come to me, where they come from, and what they hope to gain from working together. The open conversation is followed up with some structured information gathering, including the client's current job description, desired job description, elevator pitch, separation/transition story, and perceived difficulties and strengths within interviews.

From here, the conversation becomes more focused, including client-identified interview difficulties, my perceived strengths in the client, and my account of the client's growth areas (based on their Communication Profile). I must say, this conversation is always much easier than many clients anticipate it will be, as my approach to coaching is conversational and collaborative. At the conclusion of the call, the client and I have identified focus areas, action items for each of us, and a framework for setting goals in advance of the next meeting.

Executive's Communication Profile

I create what I call a "Communication Profile," which is a framework that consists of five distinct aspects pertaining to interview readiness:

1. *Mechanics — grammar and articulation*

2. *Content — quality, length, and plausibility of responses, elevator pitch, and summaries*

3. *Vocabulary — appropriate to desired position/ industry/company, positive/negative connotations*

4. *Prosody — melodic features of language, including stress, intonation, and speaking rate*

5. *Pragmatics — cultural and social cues in language.*

It is interesting how technology has changed the scope of what is considered "language" in the interview domain. Today social and cultural language norms should be considered not just in in-person interviews but also in technological interactions, including text, e-mail, phone, and web conference.

Some executives may excel in some areas and require additional support in others. The background system I use enables us to identify their strengths and development areas and create an interview style that works for them, they are comfortable with, and can use in a dynamic way to acquire the job they desire. The goal is to use our time wisely and create effective change quickly.

Developing the Executive's Communications Skills

In a variety of ways, every coach has their own approach. However, if I had to summarize my process with executives, it consists of three phases: awareness, technique, and adaptability or generalization. As a coach, it is my job to understand my executives. This not only includes their intentions for our work together and their perceived needs, but also the way they "work."

Different techniques work for different people. Referencing the client's Communication Profile, I choose the areas of biggest change and find actionable solutions. Some examples include:

- *An executive who struggles with social language difficulties like anxious leg shaking may try alternatives like moving their toes within their shoes or holding a paperclip under the desk.*

- *An executive who struggles with vocabulary that exudes confidence and positivity in their work may try a simple noun change from "we" to "I," which will make all the difference.*

- *An executive who struggles with engagement and content...now this one is a little harder. My approach often includes challenging them to decipher some of their most interesting and noteworthy stories (work, relational, and personal) to use to answer many different types of interview questions. This approach develops a conversational feel within an interview and increases listener engagement.*

Projecting a Brand in an Interview

Brand projection is the culmination of an executive's experience, character, and presentation, as well as their ability to convey this information in a meaningful, effective way. Brand recognition and identification are imperative to interview success. If an interviewer walks away without a clear picture of who the interviewee is, what they do, and their values, it means that the executive did not project their brand. Clear personal brand presentation will dictate suitability for the job for both the executive and the company.

How to Enable an Executive's Clear Messaging in an Interview

Answering the question. Plain and simple, it is important to answer the question asked. Often helping executives listen first and answer second is a skill in and of itself. The reality is, we all get nervous in interviews;

after all we are being judged (that is what an interview is). I find many times executives are so focused on one part of the question (perhaps the beginning of a long built-up question or a multi-part question) that they miss what the interviewer was actually asking, or they are so concerned about getting their great attributes highlighted they veer off topic.

Plain and simple, if you do not understand/hear the question, you cannot answer it. Given that, I work with my clients to first, listen and, second, concisely answer questions with their experience while creating an interesting, engaging response based on their communication profile and style.

Ways to Create Client Confidence

I believe all executives contain the confidence they need to achieve their goals. The aspect that is often missing is the tool(s) to show that confidence. For example, you may be the best CFO in your industry, with great experience and powerful ideas on how to impact companies from the ground up and top down. If your communication of these ideas is lackluster and your brand is unclear, the confidence is most definitely not forefront in your interviews and meetings.

Coaches work in many different ways to "create" confidence, but I often find that identifying and using an executive's strengths to tackle their development areas is the simplest and most effective approach. This creates not only a great foundation for confidence but also an excellent boost to personal brand representation.

Connecting the Written Resume to the Verbal Interview

I have often found that resumes do not match the individual in tone, presentation, and format. If your resume is composed of your highest accolades but excludes the process you pushed to get there, what good is talking about those accolades?

It is important to have a good connection to your resume, what it includes, and what it highlights, so that your interview can and will be more focused on the aspects of your career that you are proud of and/or enjoyed and that you want to talk about. Your resume should set the stage for your interview. An executive may use words like "combated," "gained," or "enlisted" to infuse emotion into their accomplishments, and start with their "how" statement to create emphasis. For example "enlisted entry-level associates to create new, relevant performance metrics, increasing company morale by 5 percent on the quarterly survey."

Simply changing the structure and presentation of the information can infuse energy, character, and personality into your resume and make you stand out. Moving on to the next experience can be intimidating, but also an exciting opportunity, and it starts with your resume.

The Two Most Common Mistakes in How Clients Have Interviewed

First, clients often come off as too nervous or too sure of themselves. This sounds contradictory, but there is a fine line in interviews, as the expectation is for the executive to answer questions and to do it well. Well, what does that mean? This is where an outside, objective perspective can be helpful. An executive could choose a trusted friend or a coach, but it is important to know how your communication is perceived.

Second, not asking enough about the company and/or potential co-workers. Let's face it, we all love to talk about ourselves. Most of us don't prefer to be in an interview when doing it, but it is one of those traits we all share. Asking about the individual across the desk from you, their experience with the company, and their perceptions of the company, can be a great way to engage your interviewer, learn more, and frankly engage in a conversation. Interviews that feel more like conversations, or where you do less of the talking, often yield better perceptions from your interviewer (because we all like to talk).

Must Hit a Home Run in an Interview?

I would say the most important aspect of an interview is authenticity. If you are authentic in the interview, the result will be what it should be. Not every company and executive are compatible and that is okay. Walking away from an interview, you should just be sure to have no regrets on how you represented yourself. Non-perfect answers and food in your teeth are not going to stop you from getting a job. Not appropriately representing your experience, qualifications, and self just might.

Bottom Line

I often tell my clients, if you are sitting in the seat (or on the phone), you are already qualified. Interviews serve as an opportunity for the company to find out more about you, and for you to find out more about the company. The interview should be thought of as a conversation and the information gleaned from that conversation is relevant to both parties. Understanding that you are looking for a great fit is just as important as the company looking for a great fit. Your experience is relevant, you are qualified, and you are also in a position to make a decision, too. This mindset often helps executives retain perspective (and treat the interview as a conversation).

Because a successful employment interview is the gateway to executive advancement, the reader's spending a little more time on Vargas' advice is warranted and well worth it.

The Salary History Question

Employers and headhunters now routinely ask for the salary history of job candidates. This was not always the case. Thirty years ago, employers would state that the position paid a certain amount and the prospective employee would accept or decline the offer or ask for a greater amount.

Salary history information has obvious advantages for the employer, especially, as often happens, when the employer has not previously revealed to the candidate what the salary for the position will be. The employer wants to pay as little as possible and will use the salary history information as the basis for its offer. This sets up an asymmetrical information advantage for the employer and does not make (to borrow an economic concept) for a "fair market valuation" of the position salary, that is, the salary a willing employee will accept from a willing employer.

Salary history screening has a discriminatory impact in keeping salaries lower than an open market would make them, that is, lower than negotiated salaries would otherwise be. For example, a woman who was out of the workforce for a few years to raise children would be disclosing outdated salary information that would be used against her in making her an offer. A usually lower-paid government employee seeking a position in the usually higher-paid private sector would be at a disadvantage. States like California, Connecticut, Delaware, Hawaii, Massachusetts, Oregon, and Vermont have already passed laws prohibiting mandatory disclosure of salary history of job applicants. Other states are gearing up to pass salary history prohibition bills.

For executives and professionals, your salary history affects your salary worth and job mobility. Consider this distortion and unfairness: You may really want a job for rational reasons and be willing to take less money, but if your salary history is high, the employer may assume you are too expensive and not even give you an interview, let alone make you an offer. If your latest salary history is low, the employer may use that against you and not offer you the higher budgeted amount for the position salary. Salary history questions are also an invasion of your personal financial privacy.

What you should say when you are asked the salary history question: "What are you currently making?" You should state why you are interested in the job opportunity and what you can contribute and that the conversation should be about is what amount the employer is willing to offer and what amount the executive is willing accept. At the same time, you should make it clear that your salary expectation is negotiable and that you are flexible. Just because a headhunter or a prospective employer asks the question, does not mean you have to answer the question, especially when it puts you at a bargaining disadvantage.

Some of my headhunter and human resources executive friends will disagree with my position on salary history information.

Headhunters

In order to get an opportunity to interview for a job, many times an executive has gone through an executive recruiter.

I have been fortunate enough to get to know fellow Amherst alumnus **Thomas Hazlett,** who has been in the high-level executive search consulting game for a couple of decades. I interviewed Tom who was kind enough to share the following observations and advice with me for the benefit of my readers.

Hazlett

Allocation of Salary versus Bonus in Compensation Packages

Performance based compensation still appears to be preferred by both hiring entities and strong executive candidates. Companies are less willing to offer large guaranteed salaries or huge signing bonuses. Performance bonus targets are being refined and more carefully calibrated. Clearly more rationality has taken hold (on both sides) in compensation negotiations.

Prevalence of Compensation in the Form of Stock or Equity

Hazlett believes the equity craze has slowed down, giving away to cash. He says, "Cash is king ... for the foreseeable future."

I counsel executives to analyze the prospects of a company in determining whether to put more emphasis on cash or equity. A huge chunk of low-value or worthless stock does the executive no good, whereas cash in hand can be used and invested.

Severance Packages

Compensation Committees of Boards of Directors are increasingly sensitive to their fiduciary duties in approving executive compensation packages. Nevertheless, according to Hazlett, "The ability to attract a crucial executive away from his or her current job, may require the offer of a substantial 'safety net' in the event of change of control or other trigger events [like executive's diminished authority and responsibilities]."

Hazlett

Three Tips for Successfully Navigating the Executive Search Process

1. *Be completely honest in every aspect of your endeavors, from resume facts, dates, compensation, degrees, etc. to answering interview questions. You must assume that everything will be checked — because it will.*

2. *Do your homework — before and during the process. Not enough due diligence about the company's situation, prospects, and agenda, and honest self-appraisal about your role, the cultural fit, and personalities of prospective colleagues can be a recipe for serious problems.*

3. *Be patient and rational during the process. This is easier to do if you are currently employed, but necessary in any case.*

Executive Coaching

An "executive coach" sounds very lofty and even mysterious to the uninitiated. I interviewed **Victor Chears**, whom I have known for many years, to shed some light on the use of executive coaches by some up-and-coming executives, as well as more established executives. Victor is the president of Chears & Associates, a firm that provides executive coaching, among other services. What follows is a primer on executive coaching.

Chears

What an Executive Coach Does

He or she works with individual leaders or leadership teams to improve their performance (much like sports coaches); provide focus or context to issues of concern; assess barriers to success; and provide a safe environment to explore strategic, personal, and operational issues that lead to effective strategies.

A primary goal of the coaching process is that leaders are more aware and better prepared to do what they do. Coaches often press buttons and push their clients to reach beyond their comfort zones.

Finding an Executive Coach

Any search should consist of careful exploration and due diligence. Practically all of my clients come from referrals and when they are introduced to me I usually talk to them extensively before we meet. That conversation consists of me exploring what they are looking for and letting them know my approach and philosophy. Therefore, I would tell someone to explore their networks to see if anyone they trust or respect has ever used a coach.

If one does go at it blind and does an Internet or association search, they should ask lots of questions and feel comfortable before proceeding.

What to Keep in Mind When Selecting an Executive Coach

Successful coaching relationships are dependent on trust, judgment, communication, mutual understanding, and goal/outcome-driven. If a person does not have a sound understanding of their own motivations and needs, a coach can take them in a direction that's based on the coach's ideas and not what the individual may actually need.

Bottom line:

Ask a lot of questions, especially behaviorally based ones like "Have you ever run across a situation like mine?" "If so, what were the outcomes?" "How long did it take?" "Was the coaching relationship successful, and define what success looked like."

The executive should get a gut feeling that allows them to make a judgment about moving to the next step.

Meaningful Certifications and Credentialing of Executive Coaches

I don't know much about the coaching websites and credentialing organizations, of which there are many. I could not advise anyone where to go from there, except to be clear on what they are looking for and see if someone's experience matches those needs.

To me the ability to be a good coach comes from a breadth of experience in a variety of situations, coupled with a keen opportunity to listen and weave what you hear with what you know in such a way that someone feels heard, served, and challenged in a positive way.

Executive Coaches Having Specialties

Many coaches come from a specialized field such as marketing and sales. Others are generalists. It actually depends on what the client is looking for in a coach. For example, many of the people that I coach are looking at making a job or career transition. I have worked with multiple leaders who have hit a "stuck" point and are asking themselves, "Is it time for a change?" or "Can I find a way to reap new satisfaction where I am?" I have had people approach me and after a conversation have let them know that I may not be the best person for them. I could give them counsel on certain levels but if they are looking for industry specialization that I don't possess, I look within my network for someone who might serve them better.

Executive Coach Differs from a Career or Business Mentor

In some instances there are no differences. What I mean is that a coach is often invested in the client in such a way that he or she is holding a specific vision for the person that they might not as yet have developed for themselves. As a result, the coach is offering counsel that could alter the course of the client's career or business.

Again, it gets back to what the person is seeking. For example, one person may be seeking a coach to improve a perceived or actual deficiency that has been highlighted by a performance appraisal or a pattern of behavior that is holding them back. Another person may want to explore coaching for a more holistic need such as whether or not they are in the right job or career.

How Executive Coaches Typically Charge and How Long Engagements Last

Fees are often dependent on the sector and the available budget. A non-profit sector executive might only be able to afford $350 an hour, while a corporate executive could pay $500+ an hour. Whether an individual is paying out-of-pocket or through the organization can also affect the pricing structure and duration. Most coaches should be able to give a general idea about the length of time involved based on stated goals and suggest a budget based on that.

Some relationships last indefinitely, as the client may seek to have the coach as a sounding board on an ongoing basis. Others want to address a specific issue or group of issues and then move on.

Knowing You Are Getting Value from Your Executive Coach

The first order of business is to have a realistic mindset about the coaching goals and to build a mutually honest and straightforward relationship. Often clients will think "I am paying you a lot of money to fix my situation," and get frustrated if things don't get "fixed" as quickly as they'd like.

An individual must resolve to be open to change, try new things, take risks, and recognize that the coach is a facilitator but not the one who is in a position to make the change occur. Now if a client follows the advice of a coach and ends up with a mess, he or she has to backtrack and look at the confluence of factors that contributed to the situation. Sometimes people are in untenable situations that, frankly, cannot be changed. A good coach will point out that the likelihood of success is slim, especially when the client is dependent on others changing in ways that will facilitate their ability to do things differently.

I have seen people walk away, frustrated, from a coaching relationship because they had unrealistic expectations (thought that the coach was going to give them a "magic bullet.") It is also crucial that the coach be honest and operate with high integrity, given the level of vulnerability a person is often in when they seek coaching.

An Example of an Executive Coaching Success Story

I recall a president of a significant non-profit organization who had a board that was dysfunctional, as in not doing their mandated jobs but rather micro-managing organizational functions that were not their purview. Further, he had board members who basically wanted him gone based on emotion rather than performance. His staff was disheartened by the dynamics that were playing out and were not functioning effectively. The day-to-day work was getting done, but basically everyone was miserable. So after we explored multiple strategies for him to effect change, it became clear that his situation was essentially unwinnable. At first that was a hard pill for him to swallow, given his long-term investment in the organization. The position had prestige and a high profile. The organization was well-known and respected in spite of the behind-the-scenes madness.

We got to a place where we both agreed that to make significant changes he would have to take a radical approach and basically "blow up everything" and take his chances at piecing together the remains — a very high-stakes and risky proposition. With that level of clarity, we began to look at alternate career possibilities and opportunities, put together a strategy for him to lay the seeds of change while seeking new options, and then transitioning out of that organization into something new. Four years later he is happier with his current career choice than his former one, and is thriving. He left with integrity and is in an environment that is supportive and rewarding.

At times my coaching was confronting his mental images of himself, but he trusted me and shifted his whole dynamic for the better.

One Last Consideration

As I noted earlier in the section on Executive Job Interview Readiness, champion golfers hire putting coaches. These golf masters are at the top of their game and yet they still know that there is always room for improvement. Why not executives? It is kind of like technology — you don't know you need it until you try it. Thirty years ago, 99 percent of the population did not have cell phones. Can you imagine not having a cell phone now? Executive coaching will be a growth business, especially as the economy improves and executives look for a competitive edge.

Reciprocal Coaching

An executive can also take a do-it-yourself approach to coaching by partnering with another person (preferably another executive) and do bi-lateral coaching.

Have you ever set personal business, career or self-improvement goals, and you look up weeks and sometimes months later not having made progress on them? You realize that you have been distracted and diverted by other challenges and tasks and your goals are in the doldrums. Career, family and extracurricular demands get in the way. Life happens.

You read, hear and know that you must set specific goals for yourself to get traction on your life's ambitions. You know further that it is preferable to have them in writing and with deadlines. You know what to do, but it is not happening.

Find a person you trust to be your coaching buddy. You hold each other's feet to the fire. You meet to discuss your goals and why you have not met them. You, of course, write them down with specific dates of completion. You check in (preferably in person) once a week with your coaching buddy and you tell each other what you have accomplished or not. Your goals may evolve over time.

What is the effect of a coaching buddy? Your knowing that you have to report to another human being on your progress toward your goals is a powerful motivator to get things done to achieve those goals. It is called accountability. What gets measured and reported gets done. It is an inexpensive way to keep you motivated and on track.

I am doing it now and it has helped to keep me focused and more on task. I do not want to come up short when I report in to my coaching buddy — a CEO — and, vice versa, nor does he. It is a simple solution. You do not need a drill sergeant or an expensive executive coach to kick you in the pants or encourage you — you just need someone to whom you made a commitment not to disappoint (other than yourself). For long range career development and holistic career counseling, an executive coach may be useful and needed. For goal setting and execution, a coaching buddy is an effective tool you ought to try.

Reciprocal coaching could work for you as it did for me and it required no financial outlay.

Networking, Ugh!

I hate the term "networking." It is a hackneyed phrase and suggests a mercenary and self-promoting activity. Most people feel networking means going to events, making small talk, collecting business cards, and promising to follow up. Other people would include informational interviews and requests for lunch or coffee as "networking." Although there is a certain randomness and hit-or-miss, scattershot quality in these approaches, the process of meeting people can be more effective and serene than that.

Purposeful and Natural

What some people call networking, I call flying your flag and meeting people. Flying your flag is seeing and being seen to let people know you exist or remind them of your presence. It is like the old famous philosophical question in solipsism: If the tree falls in the forest and makes a crashing sound and no one is around to hear it crash, does the tree make a sound? Go ponder that. Similarly, if you do not get out and about and no one sees you, how do they really know you exist? In other words, out of sight, out of mind. A certain portion of your going out and about for business reasons should be limited, strategic, and purposeful. The rest should be just a part of your daily life.

Not only do you want to meet new people, but you want to maintain connections with people whom you already know or have met. I was recently at an event where four people from the same office came together, talked together, and left together. What was that all about? I know they had families and other commitments, so why did they waste their precious time talking to each other and not promoting their organization or making connections for themselves? It possibly would have been more useful for them to have skipped the event and gone about their personal activities.

Being There and Luck Finds You

Sometimes opportunity presents itself because you happen to be at the right place at the right time. I know a guy who, when he sees me, tells people that I am responsible for his becoming a judge, because I invited him as a guest to an event at which he connected with a person who facilitated his judicial appointment. I do not even remember that particular event. However, to his point, I, too, have benefited serendipitously from attending an event like my college reunion. There a classmate learned of an area of my professional expertise and writing experience, and soon after, placed me on the editorial board of an industry magazine. Another time, as a favor, I was teaching a public speaking workshop, and an observer, unbeknownst to me, quietly recommended me as an attorney to a CEO who then called me out of the blue to represent him in his employment contract. You never know from where opportunity will come.

Some forums are better than others. Some forums are not obvious business or professional development opportunities, but abound in potential. You can develop solid relationships from your kids' school and extracurricular events and neighborhood-related activities like block and holiday parties.

An executive's going to an officially described "networking" event, I believe, is a waste of time and diminishes the executive's brand. It smacks of being a used car salesman trying to make a sale (no offense to used car salesmen). The reader can tell that I do not like the term "networking."

Now we all know of certain trade or business organizations whose major benefit is meeting people to possibly do business, but they are smart enough not to use the term "networking." People know that everyone present is there to represent or promote his or her company, firm, or business and they do so unabashedly but graciously.

Divide Your Efforts

Through trial and error, you can discern which groups, associations, or clubs seem to offer the greatest yield in terms of business, professional, or personal opportunities and information. As you have only so many hours in a day and numerous personal and work commitments, you should narrow your focus to three to four organizations that you enjoy and that prove to be productive. As for the remainder of your efforts, they should be a natural part of your social sphere like church, school, social clubs, and kids' activities. They should be natural and effortless by simply participating, being friendly, being helpful, and letting people know what you can do, but only if you are asked.

Love Thy Neighbor

Finally, be open and willing to help people when asked, with no expectation of any benefit to you. Without being preachy, this is kind of a variant of the commandment to "Love thy neighbor as thyself." The best way to love your neighbor is to help him. Even when it is inconvenient and time-consuming, it is always good for your soul to give and benefit another. Your "get" will take care of itself from some other, unexpected source, even if it just feeling great about helping another person. Having said that, you do not want to indulge a repeat favor taker (user) who never offers to help anyone else — not a good use of your time, resources, energy, and emotions. That was my long way of saying that networking should be more about being helpful to others than about seeking to help oneself. *Capiche?*

Non-Profit Boards: Why Should an Executive Bother?

You are at the upper echelon of your company or firm and have family demands making you crazy busy, and, suddenly, you are asked to join a non-profit board. Who needs it? You do, and non-profits need you.

Benefits

I have had the opportunity to sit on 10 boards. Joining a non-profit board does several things for you. It gives you boardroom experience so that you understand the organizational dynamics and etiquette of a board of directors. It gives you a chance to develop collaborative, teamwork skills with a set of usually highly accomplished peers. It gives you an opportunity to hone small group conversational and presentation skills.

If you do not already have the experience and knowledge of dealing with budgets, strategic plans, revenue generation, management performance evaluations, and public relations issues, you will likely be exposed to them sitting on a non-profit board. It gives you access to interesting people who you otherwise ordinarily would not meet, thus expanding your network. It gives you visibility. It gives you perspectives outside of the silo of your company or industry. It facilitates your contributing to a mission or cause outside your own narrow circle.

Depending on the type of organization, you invariably will enjoy some perks such as gifts of art, books, or gourmet food, free VIP tickets to performances, special briefings, retreats in posh or interesting locales, and so forth.

Things to Consider

When you are thinking about joining a board, you should do your due diligence to ascertain whether:

a) The board has competent, efficient leadership.

b) There is adequate liability insurance and/or indemnities available to protect board members.

c) There exists a conflict of interest policy.

d) The financial condition of the organization is relatively stable and manageable.

e) There is a financial contribution expectation or solicitation expectation.

Enjoy Board to Avoid Being Bored

It is important to only join boards of organizations whose missions make you feel enthusiastic and energized. You do not want to be slogging through meetings and conference calls for an organization about which you are not excited. You face an opportunity cost in doing a charitable activity (or any activity for that matter). By definition, if you are spending time doing one thing, it means you are not spending time doing another. The relative value to you of one thing to another thing must be considered.

A Nice Feather in Your Cap

There are organizations which aim to diversify for-profit corporate boards by encouraging its executive members to get meaningful non-profit board experience. Prestigious leadership programs like the competitive Leadership Greater Chicago Fellows will not usually even consider a candidate without demonstrated civic participation. I had a lunch one week with executives where we discussed the merits of serving on non-profits as preparation to serve on for-profit boards, and the consensus was that the experience is relevant and has value.

Set Limits

It is best to limit yourself to no more than two to three at a time, so that you can give total effort and not burn yourself out. Some senior executives will designate their subordinates to serve on boards in their stead. I have done this myself with younger lawyers and mentees. This is a way for companies to "groom" their up-and-coming fast-track executive stars. Similarly, as a goodwill gesture, when I do not have the time or interest to serve on a board, I usually offer to find a suitable candidate.

Do Gooder Makes Good

When all is said and done, non-profit board experience can only make you a better executive; it is an investment in both the non-profit and yourself. You do a good thing and help yourself at the same time.

Clubs, Boards, and Chicken Soup

A few years ago, my 11-year-old daughter was on spring break and accompanied me to my law offices for two days. She was my new "law firm associate." On the second day, she went with me to a luncheon board meeting at The John Marshall Law School in Chicago. The fact that there would be food and she could still read her *Chicken Soup for the Girl's Soul* book made the prospect of this meeting more palatable to her.

On the walk there she asked me, was this one of my clubs like the Economic Club of Chicago or my parish men's club? I told her "not exactly," and it surprised me that she was even aware of the Economic Club. She then asked me, "Why are you a member of clubs and organizations?" I explained to her that, like her club-lady paternal grandmother, I get a lot of satisfaction from joining, participating in, and contributing to organizations. I told her that it is important to connect with people and help people, that you cannot succeed and accomplish many things in life all by yourself, that no one is a self-made person, and that all people get help from other people along the way. It was my way of explaining the concepts of service to others and networking, all rolled into one. I also pointed out that it gives one an opportunity to socialize and stay connected with other people, a very healthy thing to do, as discussed a little later in this book.

At the meeting, my daughter saw that there was an agenda, staff made presentations, and board members discussed various topics. She saw how to run a meeting. She noted that the woman sitting next to me was an architect. When it was my daughter's turn to speak during the around-the-table introductions, at my prompting, she proudly informed the group that she wanted to become a structural engineer. She saw me and others having conversations with people after the meeting and could see that I had known some of them for many years. She could observe the old and newly made connections among the meeting participants.

My having to explain my reasons for joining clubs and serving on boards of directors gave me clarity, in the simplest terms, as to why it is meaningful to join and serve organizations. You give help, get personal gratification, and sometimes get help. It is kind of like "Chicken Soup for the Executive's Soul." Are you feeding your executive, professional soul?

TAKE-AWAY:

As I have talked to people about board service and joining clubs, one constant theme is the importance of "relationships." Nothing gets done, happens, or occurs without relationships. Whether it is business or civic or charitable pursuits, people help and do things for others based on personal human connections. No one is an island. Boards, committees, and councils all provide the social glue to get things done that an individual cannot do alone. The social capital that one invests in these leadership circles pays many dividends in personal satisfaction and effectiveness. Also, the more diverse the board, I believe, the more benefits to the organization or company in terms of perspectives, world views, and skill sets. Anecdotally, there is evidence that public companies that have more female board members increase shareholder value.

A Primer on For-Profit Corporate Board Election and Service

In talks with chairs of corporate boards of directors and executive recruiters, I have distilled 18 take-aways on corporate board service:

1. The hardest thing is to get on the first board; once you are on one, then it becomes easier to get on other boards.

2. Do not "run" for a board of directors; it is off-putting.

3. Know that you mostly get on boards because of relationships you have developed.

4. Have integrity and cultivate goodwill, which are keys to being selected for a board and being effective on a board.

5. Remember that wherever you are, you are always being observed and evaluated.

6. Do not seek to go on a board for the money; it is the wrong reason; board service well done can be time-consuming and a lot of hard work.

7. You must have some kind of experience that a board or the company can utilize.

8. Understand that just because you have the skills and expertise to be on a board does not mean you deserve to be on a board — you may not have the temperament, contacts, or reputation desired by the board chair or CEO.

9. You must immediately disassociate yourself from a CEO or a senior management team whose reputation can adversely affect your own reputation.

10. When serving, be sure to align executive compensation with the company's financial measures.

11. When you are on a board executive compensation committee, you must not look at salary and stock in isolation when making comparisons to other similarly situated CEOs; the compensation committee must look at all the compensation and benefits a CEO is receiving when comparing compensation packages.

12. If you always agree 100 percent with management and other board members, you are probably not doing your job.

13. Because shares and controlling interests can change so rapidly, a corporate director's obligation is more than just increasing shareholder value; other stakeholders, like employees, vendors, customers, and communities should also be taken into account.

14. Be prepared for each board meeting.

15. Attend board meetings.

16. Do go on a board because you believe in the company and have something to contribute.

17. Listen first, and listen more than you speak.

18. Do not put anything on the agenda without already knowing what the voting outcome will be.

The Efficacy of Holiday Greeting Cards

In our high-tech electronic age, sending holiday greeting cards through the mail may seem antiquated. Electronic holiday cards with lots of bells, whistles, and graphics appear more and more every year. Despite my law firm's new sophisticated contact system, my getting my holiday cards out has only gotten slightly easier and a little less time-consuming.

Every year I face the same questions: Who should get a card? Does it matter? Will my card even be noticed in the flood of holiday mail? Is the time spent justified? Is the cost justified? Am I forgetting somebody? Am I killing a tree or two to create the paper greeting cards and envelopes? Should I use electronic greeting cards?

I still come down on the side that the time and expense of sending cards is worth it. It is, indeed, a pain in the neck keeping addresses current. I would guess that every year there is a 15 percent change in addresses arising from job changes, residential moves, and, sadly, from death. Invariably, I will forget to include someone who should be on my list. I am sure most of my cards get buried in the crush of holiday mail, but I do get a couple of people who mention they got my card or e-mail me that they did and that they appreciate the recognition. I value their acknowledgement and it makes my efforts feel worthwhile.

My main purpose for sending out cards on my business and personal mailing list is to let people know that I am thinking of them and to stay in touch, even if it is just once a year. I learned this staying-in-touch rationale from my mother. A physical card is a more concrete, satisfying way to reach out to someone than a global broadcast of an update on Facebook or LinkedIn or an e-mail blast.

I do not mind receiving electronic holiday cards, as some of them can be quite clever and artistic. I might even start sending them myself one day.

For the last end-of-the-year holiday season, I sent out Thanksgiving cards to avoid my cards getting overlooked in the crush of the regular winter holiday mail. It is a way to mix it up and to have my cards stand out. Fourth of July cards is another option to consider in order to get the biggest bang for my greeting card buck so to speak. Your getting creative with your communications to your network should be an ongoing process.

Ideally, I would love to be able to write a note to everyone on my list, but the time spent doing it would take me to next Christmas, and so I have to be content with just signing my cards. Sometimes, I will sneak a note into one of my cards when I have a compelling sentiment.

Is it mandatory for an executive or professional to send out holiday cards? It is a nice touch. People will certainly remember if and how well you did something for them more than the fact that you sent them a holiday card. A card is neither the cake nor the icing, but a nice sprinkle on the icing. If you can find the time, then do it.

Thank You Notes and Other Missives

There is a lot written about the importance of writing thank-you notes and how people do not write them often enough or do not write them at all. The lack of writing extends to congratulatory notes, get-well notes, and condolence notes. There are countless articles written on how you must write a thank-you note after a job interview and how such an act will distinguish one from other job candidates. Seems pretty basic, doesn't it? The fact is that fewer and fewer people hand-write anything, let alone missives that have to be sent by snail mail. Brad, a neighbor of mine who is an executive recruiter and with whom I was having a lunch, mentioned that his first boss instructed him to go and get bond paper stationary with his name printed on it. Puzzled, Brad asked, "Why?" His boss said, "You need to take the time and show people your appreciation by handwritten notes." My neighbor gets it.

My own mother, Louise, brainwashed my siblings and me that basic etiquette required one to write a thank-you note for everything ranging from receiving gifts to staying as a guest in someone's home to benefiting from a recommendation. So I do write a lot of thank-you notes and other notes, but I feel I still do not write enough of them. I need to be more compulsive about it.

President George H.W. Bush reportedly was an inveterate note writer. I suspect it had to do with his old-school Yankee upbringing, where etiquette was part of "proper" training. His sending notes to folks may have given him that little extra edge that made him a Congressman, an Envoy to China, a CIA Director, a UN Ambassador, a Vice President, and, ultimately, a President of the United States.

What about thank-you e-mails? What about thank-you text messages? What about thank-you voice-mails or phone calls? They are all good, and vindicate the principle of expressing gratitude. A handwritten thank-you note is more personal and makes a bigger impact on the receiver. I know when I receive a handwritten note, I do notice.

It takes a lot of effort to be conscientious about writing and sending notes. It is worth the effort of letting people know that you appreciate, value, and acknowledge them. Isn't that what life is all about — making those human connections as often as we can? Now I will go and remind my son to mail his note to his godmother, thanking her for his birthday present. He will be writing them of his own volition soon.

Being There

I went to a funeral of the mother of a friend. I took my then nine-year-old son with me, as he was hanging out with me this day at my law offices during his spring break. He had only been to two previous funerals, one for his cousin and one for his maternal grandfather.

"Papa," he asked, "why are we going to this funeral so far away and who is this person?" It was only 19 miles away, but to him, it seemed to be in another state.

I explained to him that a friend's elderly mother died and I wanted to show her and her family my support. She had always been supportive of me. I told my son that you have to be there for people and "show up for them." It is part of being a gentleman, being compassionate, and being gracious. "That's what we do," I said. He understood. Although he was having fun watching videos in my office before we left for the funeral, he got it that doing the right thing always comes ahead of self-centeredness and inconvenience.

In life, as in business, small gestures of compassion and kindness count. My having to explain to my son the importance of showing up for friends and colleagues reinforced for me the importance of being there for others. I endeavor to always be counted upon when it counts. I hope my son tries, too.

CHAPTER SIX

EXECUTIVE RESILIENCE AND REINVENTION

Resilience

"Victory belongs to the most persevering."

~Napoleon Bonaparte

A few years ago, as a Christmas present to ourselves, my wife and I went to a spa after New Year's Day to start the year with vim and vigor. I got an 80-minute massage from a masseuse who told me her life story of child abuse, a broken home, single parenthood, homelessness, and a broken neck in a car accident. She told me how through sheer willpower she had rebounded back to being self-sufficient and taking care of her 13-year-old son. As I tell my kids, what happens to you is not as determinative as how you choose to respond to what happens to you. It sounds like a cliché, but it is absolutely true.

Despite the grim parts, her story got me thinking about executives who survive adversity and those who do not. If I had to pick a single character trait that distinguishes exceptional executives and professionals from the not-so-great ones, it would be "resilience." In short, the terrible challenges that the masseuse had overcome, and her upbeat, "can do" perspective on life, was a clarion call to me that despite whatever setback, failure, pain, and suffering one has endured, the trait of resilience is essential to a person's recovery and success.

In my observations from my executive advisory perch, what stands out is that the ability to persevere in the face of setbacks, reverses, failures, and adverse circumstances is essential to any long-term career and business success. And yes, there are second, third, and even fourth acts if you have the tenacity to recover. Remember the setbacks suffered by Jamie Dimon of JPMorgan Chase, Richard Grasso of the New York Stock Exchange, and Steve Jobs of Apple. Comebacks are the stuff of legends, especially in American culture.

Even the *Wall Street Journal*, in its 29 April, 2008, Health Journal column, noted in its headline, "If at First You Don't Succeed, You're in Excellent Company." The columnist, Melinda Beck, cited the setbacks and successes of Julie Andrews, J. K. Rowling, Walt Disney, Michael Jordan, and the Beatles. She noted the trait of self-efficacy, that is, "the unshakable belief some people have that they have what it takes to succeed." So with that in mind, do you believe in your capabilities? Can you rebound and climb back to even greater achievements? I dare say most executives have not experienced as much adversity as that masseuse. If she could rebound, why not you or I? Mind over matter, as we see in the next chapter on health and productivity.

Reinvention

My wife and I went to another spa, and there my young masseur's story of his work trajectory revealed his reinvention and adaptability. He was from the Detroit area and had never finished college. He had picked up some IT skills and got a job working for Accenture in Chicago doing automated payroll process consulting. He felt Chicago offered cosmopolitan excitement and economic opportunity that Detroit could not. He worked crazy hours and made good money. He was a very young 20-something who did not like the work stress and office politics. When his department functions were being moved to San Antonio, he decided not to move, took a severance package, and trained to be a massage therapist. Although he likes his job and his less pressured lifestyle, he intends eventually to go to school to become a physical therapist. It will take him five years to get a master's degree. He knows there is job growth in health care. His father, a railroad retiree, does not understand his desire to change careers every few years.

This young adult represents the realities of the new economy and alternative career paths. He knows instinctively that he has to keep reinventing himself and be mobile. He does not resent this fact; this is all he has ever known in his short career.

He is not an executive or highly educated professional, but his situation is instructive. We must all reinvent ourselves and become adaptable in order to continue to be useful and relevant in the marketplace. A person who remains static will eventually be out of a job or lose her business. Whole professions and industries have already been disrupted: stock brokerage, real estate brokerage, publishing, retail, journalism, health care, academia, the legal profession, and so forth. Old kinds of jobs are disappearing and new job descriptions are being created every day.

In my own case, I am glad that 20 years ago, as a result of my parttime appointment as an Illinois Human Rights Commissioner, I became involved in employment legal matters, even though I had been primarily a business and real estate attorney. So as the real estate and construction industries cratered during the Great Recession, my long-ago diversification into executive employment contracts benefited my law practice. This "reinvention" and my longtime receptivity and relatively early adaptability to new technology like laptops, the Internet, and social media (I know I must sound ancient to some young folk) have kept me relevant and in the game over the years. This all, to be sure, is the result of a combination of serendipity and purposefulness.

My take-aways from the young man is that, first, reinvention is constant and seems to be accelerating, and, second, learning how to learn prepares one well for a rapidly changing economy and workplace. Knowledge becomes obsolete very quickly. This whole phenomenon reminds me of one of my father's favorite admonitions: "Don't rest on your laurels."

CHAPTER SEVEN

HEALTH AND PRODUCTIVITY

Habit One — Exercise

About four years ago, my wife and I began running or doing weight machines every day, rain or shine. We exercise every single day, sometimes together and sometimes separately, depending on our schedules. I do more running outside than doing machines at the gym. My wife prefers the gym. I do mine religiously at 5:00 a.m. I try to run or walk at least three miles or at least for an hour. I know that if I do not get the exercise done in the morning, it will not get done, as professional demands, kids' activities, and life get in the way. I am not a natural fan of running (I prefer hiking) and I am a sleepy-head. When the alarm goes off, I do not allow myself to think I have the choice to stay in bed, and I just get up.

Importantly, the early morning start prepares me mentally and physically for the rest of the day.

I have found the following benefits from this exercise regimen:

- My day is more orderly.

- I am more mentally alert throughout the day.

- I have much more stamina for a long day.

- I have a higher tolerance for stressful stimuli.

- I have a greater disposition for feeling cheerful.

- My capacity to maintain my calm and tranquility is greatly enhanced.

- My sundry aches and pains have disappeared.

- I get more tasks and events accomplished.

I certainly have not discovered anything new in terms of what contributes to a more efficient, productive, and enjoyable day. If you survey the literature on the attributes of modern, high-achieving executives and leaders, you will see that a high percentage of them exercise frequently.

Give yourself a lift, and start exercising every day. Oh, and did I mention that you will probably lose weight and firm up your body in the process? Hard work, but lots of payoffs.

Habit Two — Sleep

Like many erstwhile self-imposed Type-A Personality workaholics, I would burn the candle at both ends making myself feel self-important and indispensable. Of course, the result was sleep deprivation. Several years ago, I started seeing a lot of articles and reports about the ill effects of insufficient sleep. Lack of sleep has many real-life health consequences, like weight gain/obesity, cognitive impairment, heart problems, high blood pressure, stroke, diabetes, and shortened life span, among other bad things. It seemed counterintuitive as to weight loss. One would expect to burn more calories the less still one is. However, lack of sleep tends to lead to weight gain; apparently sleep affects metabolism. Sleep deprivation obviously impacts cognitive functions and moods. We know fatigued drivers cause accidents and sleepy babies become fussy. We know sustained sleep deprivation is used as a form of torture. A more recent study suggests people who get insufficient sleep knock off a few years from their lives.

In analyzing my mental agility and stamina in relation to the number of hours I slept in a night, I discerned that five hours of sleep was not enough and eight hours of sleep was optimal. I resolved to get a good night's sleep every night when possible. I turn into a pumpkin around 10:00 p.m. anyway, so keeping this resolution was easy to do. What happened? I have become a true believer. The additional hours of sleep resulted in my:

- Being more alert throughout the day
- Being more productive
- Having more stamina
- Having a sustained cheerful mood
- Getting sick less often
- Having more energy to exercise
- Having a higher tolerance for stressful stimuli

These benefits are substantially symmetrical to the benefits noted in the earlier discussion about exercise. Sufficient sleep and sufficient exercise are two sides of the same coin, both contributing to overall physical and mental well-being. This well-being provides a foundation to maximize one's overall performance at work and at play.

Although they talk about how busy they are, most executives and professionals do not talk about how much sleep they get. They may mention going to bed late, getting up in the middle of the night, waking early, or "sleeping in" on a weekend day. You usually do not hear people quantifying the average number of hours they sleep each night. So it is hard to know what effective leaders are doing in terms of enough sleep. Of course, people are variable, so I expect each individual's need for sleep or each individual's tolerance for insufficient sleep will also be variable.

I suspect everyone has an optimal number of hours of sleep that is his or her sweet spot in well-being. What's yours? I know my night-owl wife needs less sleep than I. Seven to eight hours feels right for my constitution.

In any event, I can corroborate that the literature on the salutary effects of sufficient sleep is correct. A good night's sleep makes me better at what I do.

Habit Three — Meditation, Prayer, or Stillness

Contemplative practice or spirituality or both are additional habits that contribute to resilience. This habit maybe a little tricky for those who may not be spiritual or who are atheists. You do not need to be either spiritual or atheistic. You can be contemplative and reap the same calming, connectedness, and perspective-giving benefit.

For me, I pray every day. Most days I meditate as the spirit moves me or convenience presents itself.

I remember reading years ago some of Sigmund Freud's writings and I believe he made the observation that one of his male patients could benefit psychologically from practicing his religion and deepening his religious faith.

I do know that Freud said in his *New Introductory Lectures on Psychoanalysis:* "If one wishes to form a true estimate of the full grandeur of religion, one must keep in mind what it undertakes to do for men. It gives them information about the source and origin of the universe, it assures them of protection and final happiness amid the changing vicissitudes of life, and it guides their thoughts and motions by means of precepts which are backed by the whole force of its authority."

Freud's observation about his patient always struck me as true, and when I started doing just that many years later, I found it to be true, in fact, for me personally. I am not as religious as I could be, but I try to adhere to my religion as much as possible and I seek spirituality. Religion can provide a lot of comfort.

I am Roman Catholic and I say a prayer of my own authorship as well as the standard "Our Father" and "Hail Mary." I try to pray twice a day, in the morning and at night. Invariably, I wake up in the middle of night and that is when I usually meditate. Sometimes I meditate while jogging, sometimes while driving, sometimes while riding my commuter train, and sometimes while at work. My meditation is breath focused or sometimes reciting a mantra; the idea is to empty my brain of noise and runaway, random thoughts. During the day, I try to have a few minutes of just being still and silent. I do that most often in my big leather club chair in our master bedroom.

Now there is much research that substantiates the health effects of relaxation methods. No less august medical institutions than the Mayo Clinic and Massachusetts General Hospital's Benson-Henry Institute for Mind Body Medicine have corroborated the healthful benefits of meditation to relieve stress, reduce pain, and combat disease. More and more employers — like Google and General Mills — are encouraging their employees to meditate. These employers believe meditation positively affects their bottom line through employee wellness, productivity and cognitive enhancement.

Even as little as five minutes a day could have huge benefits for you. And your meditation sessions do not have to be perfect: You may have a million distracting thoughts intruding, but as long as you keep returning to concentrating on your breathing or mantra, you are achieving a benefit, whether it is immediate or delayed.

I have found that these practices have restorative effects and gird me for whatever challenges that may arise during a particular day. I have observed that my friends who are devout Jews, Muslims, Hindus, or Christians, or serious meditators seem, on average, to have calmer temperaments and more equanimity than others.

Spiritual prayers or meditative practices contribute to a state of being that can be capsulized in one word: "calm." Is there a better state in which to live?

As the Dalai Lama reminds us, "If you are calm, even your enemy cannot disturb you."

Are you stressed out? Burned out? Is your resilience down? Prayer and/or meditation may help to provide the antidote you need.

Five Helpful Books on Meditation and Spirituality

1. *The Power of Now: A Guide to Spiritual Enlightenment* by Eckhart Tolle

2. *Wherever You Go, There You Are: Mindfulness Meditation in Everyday Life* by Jon Kabat-Zinn

3. *10% Happier: How I Tamed the Voice in My Head, Reduced Stress Without Losing My Edge, and Found Self-Help That Actually Works — A True Story* by Dan Harris

4. *How to Practice: The Way to a Meaningful Life* by Dalai Lama and Jeffrey Hopkins

5. *The Joy of Living: Unlocking the Secret and Science of Happiness* by Yongey Mingyur Rinpoche and Eric Swanson

Habit Four — Social Networks

Another salutary habit that contributes to resilience is socializing.

Social networks are key to well-being. Do you have friends? Do you have a family that is both accessible and supportive? Do you belong to groups and participate in them? Human beings are social creatures who evolved and survived well because of their social organizing instincts that provided protection, hunting, food-gathering and cultivation, division of labor, and trade, among so many other things.

My mother, Louise, was a club lady. All of her adult life she was a joiner of social and civic clubs, had lots of friends, and was devoted to her family. In return, her friends, club members, and family were devoted to her. She was cheerful, strong, and tenacious. She embodied resilience. No question that her socializing enhanced her resilience both physically and emotionally.

I get my "joiner" and "civic" genes from my mother. I guess I am a club guy (no, not the bar kind). I am a member of four men's clubs: a church club, two social clubs, and a professional fraternity. I have also sat on several boards and commissions and volunteer a lot.

What I have found is that, like my mother, I get strength and energy from my social networks. The time I spend in my clubs and civic activities uplifts me, gives me energy, and relaxes me. If you are socializing or serving others, you do not have much time to brood or feel sorry for yourself. In fact, friendship, family, and civic ties armor you from the slings and arrows of outrageous fortune (to borrow a phrase from Shakespeare). No matter what real or imagined slights, setbacks, failures, or mistakes befall you, they all become much more manageable when you have a strong social network. Your friends, neighbors, colleagues, and family provide the empathy, encouragement, support, and suggestions to propel you through the inevitable ups and downs of your life.

Whenever there is a death or a serious illness of a neighbor's loved one, my Chicago neighborhood erupts in an outpouring of emotional and practical support. The bereaved or distressed family does not have to cook for at least a couple of weeks. It is a beautiful thing to see. That kind of social network enhances resilience.

Selective solitude can be extremely satisfying and sometimes necessary. Sustained aloneness without meaningful social ties can be harmful.

Strong social support networks contribute to good health and longevity. Dynamic, effective leaders are social and have extensive networks.

Have you taken stock of your network lately? Do you tend to your nuclear and/or extended family, keep up with your friends, and engage with others in your community? It is never too late to start. A smile, a hello, and a willingness to roll up your sleeves are all you need to tap into the social being you are meant to be. When was the last time you called a friend for no reason or had a random lunch with no agenda and or sent an e-mail or text "just because"?

Habit Five — Setting Goals

"Just as your car runs more smoothly and requires less energy to go faster and farther when the wheels are in perfect alignment, you perform better when your thoughts, feelings, emotions, goals, and values are in balance."

~Brian Tracy

Without goals, the journey of life becomes aimless, wandering and meaningless. When studies have been done on groups and individuals who live long lives, one characteristic that stands out is having a purpose in life, that is, a reason to get out of bed every day. Whether it is to accomplish household tasks, treat one's patients, counsel one's client's, serve one's customers, take care of one's family member, teach a child, write a book, or something else, a person must have goals, whether they are small or big, short- or long-term. As pointed out earlier in this book, one's obtaining a buddy to do reciprocal coaching is a way to drive oneself toward achieving one's goals.

My mother's goals were to see her grandchildren raised well, become highly educated, have professional jobs, and marry a quality person. She also wanted to live to be 100 to see these goals accomplished by her progeny. She was two and a half months shy of her hundredth birthday when she passed away. These goals motivated my mother to look forward every day to hear from and engage with her children and grandchildren. She never stopped thinking about her progeny realizing their potential in terms of character development and achievement.

In looking back over my life, the goal I set of becoming a practicing lawyer when I was 15 years old informed my decisions and efforts for many years. More recently, for five years, I had the goals of canoeing the Minnesota/Canadian Boundary Waters and backpacking at the Philmont Scout Ranch in New Mexico with my Boy Scout son, Max. These arduous scouting adventure goals kept me motivated to get in physical shape and stay deeply involved in scouting as an adult leader.

Many years ago, I had also set a long-term goal of writing a book. I was not certain what the topic would be, but I knew I wanted to write a book. I thought the simplest way would be for me to start a blog and churn out pithy articles, one at a time, so that I could eventually collect and edit these articles into a book. I would write about what I was interested in and what I knew about. I knew I could accomplish the small bite goals of individual articles in order to achieve the swallowing of the huge goal of writing a book. And here I am, writing my book on executive employment and development matters that is substantially derived from my blogging.

In looking back, I realize, that, among other goals, the goals of becoming a lawyer, doing scouting high adventures, and writing a book were healthy outlets for me and contributed to a higher day-to-day quality of life. Plain and simple, purpose gives meaning to life, and goals help to establish purpose. Of course, there is psychic satisfaction in accomplishing goals. What is your bucket list? The items on your list need not be grandiose, just something you want to do and that you will follow through on. You will find that setting and working toward goals enhances all areas of your life. My latest goal? Learn Spanish by using a smart phone language app for 15 minutes a day. This daily task is realistic and do-able. Eat the elephant, one small bite at a time. *Es cierto?*

Age Is Just a Number

"Some men never seem to grow old. Always active in thought, always ready to adopt new ideas, they are never chargeable with fogyism. Satisfied, yet ever dissatisfied, settled, yet ever unsettled, they always enjoy the best of what is, and are the first to find the best of what will be."

~William Shakespeare

Epiphany in the Mountains of New Mexico

One of my best friends, Craig, is a 50-something entrepreneur who pioneered energy conservation consulting before it became mainstream and cool. He and I both have sons in Boy Scouts and he had just returned from a two-week high adventure, backpacking trek at the Philmont Scout Ranch in New Mexico. I am talking about mountains, bears, mountain lions, hot days, cold nights, lots of thunderstorms, and serious hiking. Philmont equates to a Boy Scout Disneyland for scouts and their adult leaders. It is a once-in-a-lifetime experience, although some participants go back multiple times.

Craig did a lot of thinking about life, family, and business during his challenging hikes and camping and he kept a journal. As soon as he got back to Chicago, Craig excitedly called me up and said, "Let's have lunch so I can do a mind dump on some insights I developed out in New Mexico."

At lunch he said, "People are living much longer nowadays. Look at our own long-lived family members. Medical advances and nutrition make the odds of our living to be at least 100 years very high. That means, G. A., we have to rethink how we approach the arc of our lives and what we do with it. Our lives have three chunks of active, productive time or phases: zero to 30; 31 to 60, and 61 to 90. Our children can have three separate, different experiences in their lives and you and I have one more major one left. Isn't that great? We have much more time to do and experience different things, including work."

From our long conversations, Craig and I realized that we could turn down several notches the day-to-day striving, driving stress of retirement nest-egging and personal achievements and fear about the road not taken, because we had a good 30-plus more years to do it. Life was not as short as we thought, as there was so much more each of us can do, assuming that we benefit from the increasing longevity trend. We could explore and accomplish many new things. I had always thought that the idea of retirement in one's 50s or 60s when one was at the peak of one's experience, knowledge, expertise, and skills was absurd. Now I think disengaging even in one's 70s is nonsensical.

This insight was recently brought home to me when I attended a summer soiree at the home of my friend and mentor James D. Montgomery, Sr., a prominent and prosperous 85-year-old Chicago attorney, who was a law partner with Los Angeles-based Johnny Cochran of O.J. Simpson fame. I asked Jim how his law business was going and he said, "It's going great and I am working on my legacy." Jim looks 20 years younger than his age. He further remarked that continuing to practice law contributed to his health and vitality.

More Evidence: The Age of Entrepreneurs — It's Not What You Expect

I serve on an advisory board of a small company and the president of this company asked me to attend her inauguration as a member of the second cohort class for Goldman Sachs 10,000 Small Businesses in Chicago. This is an initiative driven by Goldman Sachs and its local partner, City Colleges of Chicago, to generate economic growth and job creation through small businesses by facilitating their access to business education, financial capital, and business support services.

As I watched the recently graduated first cohort members speak about their exceptional experiences in the program and the second cohort members speak about their dreams, aspirations, and ambitions, I was struck by the ages of these eager entrepreneurs. Yes, there were several 20-somethings and 30-somethings, but a large number were in middle and advanced middle age. Some had been in business for 35 years and some had MBAs. My friend Craig was right about the reality of the third productive phase of life, if you choose it.

What did this plurality of older entrepreneurs show me? It showed me that enthusiasm, energy, motivation, and achievement cannot be limited by age. It reminded me that when you stop growing and learning, then you are in decline. You are done. Asian and African cultures put a premium on age and wisdom. In the U.S., we have become defined and intimidated by a youth-obsessed culture. As Henry Ford observed, "You take all the experience and judgment of men over fifty out of the world and there wouldn't be enough left to run it."

Continuous Learning

The fact is that you do not really hit your stride until middle age in terms of competence, confidence, and knowledge. Middle age and older are the stages in life when you begin to reap the dividends of your experience and skill sets. Most important, though, is to continue to broaden your experience and expand your skill sets. You must always be in learning mode.

My mother exemplifies the learning mindset, in that she went back to college in her late 50s and she was always intellectually and socially curious. I also saw this energetic mindset when I attended the dedication of a courthouse in honor of retired federal Judge George Leighton, who practiced law until he was 98 and died at 105 years of age. A Grand Master, Judge Leighton had played chess every day to keep his mind sharp, even if he had to do it online from his computer.

Maturity as an Asset and an Advantage

As we see with Jim Montgomery and Judge Leighton, there is much human capital in older executives, entrepreneurs, and professionals that can and needs to be continuously exploited. Our nation cannot afford not to use this older human capital to leverage and grow our economy. I am comforted to see that older hands are helping to drive the entrepreneurial spirit in our small businesses. I will be as delighted to see when older, experienced hands remain in the executive and professional suites using their talents to push our economy forward. I have represented too many male and female executives who are pushed out the executive door in their 50s. I am glad my own law firm embraces and practices utilizing older talent — that philosophy has helped our firm thrive. Our clients value the experienced, seasoned attorney who does not have a learning curve concerning their urgent problems.

No matter how old you are, as long as you can do it, you should be on "the hunt" for business and professional development, success, and achievement.

CHAPTER EIGHT

THINGS AN EXECUTIVE OUGHT TO KNOW AND DO

Customer Service, Names, and Politeness: Executive Lessons from my Dry Cleaning Lady

One Saturday I walked into a dry cleaner's with a pile of clothes at three minutes before closing time. I walked out with three lessons. First, the power of customer service. Second, the power of remembering names. Third, the power of politeness.

Customer Service

When I walked in with a big load just before five o'clock on a sweltering day, the owner of the shop did not groan or give me a pained look, although clearly she had gone through a long, grueling day. In fact, she mentioned cheerfully how busy she had been. The dry cleaning owner could have said we're closed or given me a sour-puss facial expression.

How many business books and advertisers out there talk about putting the customer or client first? Plenty. How many executives and professionals actually do? Not nearly enough. I left my previous dry cleaning lady because she charged me to replace two buttons that her dry cleaning process damaged in the first place — no customer service there.

Forget Me Not

The dry cleaning owner finished taking care of the customer before me and then attended to me. She knew my name, although I had only been there four times in a nine-month period. I asked her did she use mnemonic techniques to remember people's names. She said no and mentioned that many of her customers asked her how she remembered their names. I asked her how she did it and why. She said, "I make a great effort to remember a customer's name, and after the second time I see the person, I force myself to think hard." She went on further to say, "I do it because I am the owner of my business, not an employee, and it is important to know my customers." The dry cleaning owner could have chosen not to make the effort to remember my name.

A former colleague of mine told me a story about how the late Chicago Mayor Richard J. Daley, a Democrat, met him once and never forgot his name upon subsequent meetings — that made a huge, positive impression on my colleague, a Republican. Self-improvement guru Dale Carnegie said there is no sweeter sound to a person than to hear his own name. It is true.

Good Manners

While I was counting out my many shirts, she asked me whether I would mind her taking care of the woman behind me who had come to pick up a very small batch of dry cleaning. I said no problem. The dry cleaning owner could have helped the other customer behind me without asking for my permission.

Our mothers stressed good manners as a way of being gracious and smoothing social interaction. How often do we forget to show even basic manners? I heard actor Robert Duvall repeatedly say "yes sir" or "no sir" to a radio interviewer and those simple, polite replies endeared him to the audience. The dry cleaning lady had made a point to ask my permission before waiting on the other customer. Manners do matter.

Every day there are wonderful lessons and reminders all around us of how to be better executives and better people. Now if I can just get rid of my brain cramps and start remembering people's names.

Trust: Executive Lessons from My Auto Repair Lady

Several years ago I went to an auto body shop recommended by my auto insurer to get a driver's-side mirror replaced. The young lady who runs her family business was efficient and cheerful and gave me a reasonable estimate. She drove me to and from my commuter rail station so I did not have to worry about cabbing it. The shop finished the job quickly and expertly.

My wife's car eventually needed some auto body repair work and she received the same treatment. We learned that the shop also did regular auto repairs and decided to give the shop a try. For both our cars, the auto body shop's mechanical repairs were cheaper than our auto dealer's. In terms of our treatment, the shop was consistently friendly, efficient, and reasonable in cost. Now we don't take our cars to be repaired anywhere else. My wife and I have watched that young lady get married, have two children, and continue to run the family business with the help of her husband and parents.

A Used Car?

The other day, while I was being driven home from the auto body shop, the young lady mentioned that her family business was now also selling pre-driven cars, that is, used cars. She told me that her criterion for selling a car was simply that she would only sell a car that she herself would buy.

Now I had never bought a used car and did not think I ever would in my life. Now if I have the need, I would buy a used car from this young lady. Why is that? Trust! I trust her and her business. Over the years, by her consistent conduct and consistent service, she has earned my family's business trust. So much so that I have altered my risk-averse policy of never buying a used car. Our business relationship has evolved from body work to mechanical repairs and now to used car sales. It reminds me of the old saw on ultimate trustworthiness: "Would you buy a used car from this guy?"

What Has Trust Got To Do With It?

Executives, entrepreneurs, and professionals are often so focused on "making the sale" and delivering the good or service that they forget the fundamental glue in a business transaction or business relationship is establishing and maintaining trust.

Consumers trust Apple products because they know the products will be consistently fun, useful, high quality, and cutting edge. Fast-food diners trust McDonald's because they know the food and drink will be consistently cheap, filling, and flavorful (sugary, salty, and fatty) and most times served in a clean restaurant. Coffee drinkers trust Starbucks because they can expect the baristas to know their preferences and they can linger as though they were in a European café. These consumers know exactly what they are getting and they, in turn, become receptive to new product offerings of these companies, whether it be an iPad, a McRib sandwich, or instant coffee. Do your customers or clients or patients know what they are getting? Do they trust what they are getting?

Consistent good conduct and service create trust. So, too, executives and professionals must put first and foremost their trustworthiness in the delivery of their goods and services and in their personal behavior.

Trust as a Soft Skill

I have always naturally focused on competence and reliability, and I never consciously thought about the importance of the trust factor. When my clients keep coming back to me for strategic career or corporate advice, even long after I have negotiated their employment contracts or severance packages or drafted their LLC operating agreements, I now understand it is because they trust me.

Without trust, an executive or a professional cannot do long-term business effectively. We know trust when we feel it.

Are you trusted in business? Do your colleagues trust you? Do your customers, clients, or patients trust you? It is unfortunate that our graduate schools and professional schools don't teach a course on trust. This soft trait/skill is our most important one.

In discussing this subject with my friend John, he made a keen observation that got me thinking: the idea that it is important for leaders to trust their customers, colleagues, and direct reports — that it is a two-way street. In order to gain trust, you must also give it. It reminds me of the newsstand guy on the first floor of my office building, who tells his customers "pay me later" when they are short of change for a couple of candy bars. They always pay him and usually go to him rather than the cheaper drugstore down the street.

In another discussion with my late friend Cory, we focused on the observation that consistently meeting and exceeding expectations is critical to building trust with customers, bosses, employees, and family members. I mentioned that I had naturally focused on competence and reliability and had not thought consciously about trust. I was doing the right things, but did not understand their positive outcome: trustworthiness. Your explicit prescription for positive behavioral consistency in meeting and exceeding expectations is a great guide toward achieving trust.

In a *Wall Street Journal* article on August 29, 2011, called "Playing Favorites," reporter Melissa Korn noted that managers acknowledge playing favorites influences their decision-making in granting promotions and that, while checks and balances are utilized to be fair, things like evaluating job-related skills and using multiple interviewers, managers also used "more subjective criteria, including trustworthiness and comfort working with an employee."

So while technical prowess may be a required skill set, its delivery must be consistent in order to build trust. There are vendors and service providers who may not have warm and fuzzy personalities, but we trust them because of the way they consistently deliver their products and services.

Employee Appreciation as Good Business

Effective organizations celebrate their employees' contributions. Better yet — highly effective organizations celebrate their employees, *period*. Again, I learn from my auto repair lady.

As mentioned earlier in this book, the young woman who manages her family's auto repair business invited my family to attend the company's 25th Anniversary Celebration Picnic. My then 10-year-old son, Max, and I went to the picnic in Lincolnwood, a close-in Chicago suburb. In attendance were the company's important customers, vendors, and employees.

There was plenty of food and free raffle prizes. After an introduction by his daughter on the beginnings of the business, the founding father gave a short speech in Korean. The primary focus of his remarks and the beneficiaries of certain special prizes were the employees. Daughter and father knew that their prospects for the family business very much depended on their hardworking and dedicated employees. They communicated simply and repeatedly how the employees were responsible for the success of the business. The long tenure of the multi-ethnic employees spoke volumes about how the employees felt about their employer. The employees were relaxed and comfortable and seemed like an extended family at a reunion. What executive would not want his employees to feel the same way?

Successful business people and leaders of organizations, large or small, for-profit or non-profit, or governmental, know that people want to feel valued. Sure, monetary compensation and benefits are important, too, but knowing that your managers appreciate you has great psychological value. No one likes to feel invisible or inconsequential. Too often the attitude of managers, especially in fast-moving, sometimes challenging economic times, is that the employee ought to be glad she has a job and not complain. I get the managers' perspectives, but they need to also understand that unhappy employees usually are not the most productive employees.

Employers do themselves, their customers, clients, and stakeholders a huge favor when they make their employees happy. Appropriate recognition of, and earned, deserved positive feedback to employees, will contribute to employees' contentment, and become fundamental to a healthy enterprise. Investments of praise, appreciation, and recognition for genuine employee achievements will reap enormous dividends for both the employee and the enterprise.

Celebration for its own sake also creates returns to the organization. Every month at my law firm, we celebrate with ice cream cakes those owners and staff who have birthdays. Just because.

When an executive's superiors acknowledge her achievements, then that should remind and prompt her, in turn, to recognize her subordinates' contributions. Recognition and acknowledgment of an employee as a valued member of the enterprise or as simply a valued human being does not necessarily have to be as a result of a work-related contribution or an achievement.

Positive feedback and a positive environment does not have to be expensive, it just has to be earnest and authentic. Continual, earned positive feedback to employees is yet another executive lesson from my auto repair lady.

Management Succession Planning: Be Like a Boy Scout and Be Prepared

An executive client recently asked for advice concerning creation of a management succession plan. Given the tragedy of 9/11 and the inevitability of things like natural disasters, such a request for assistance is always prudent and timely.

Who Is Doing Succession Planning?

I was at a breakfast seminar where the topic was "evaluating board members" and it was pointed out by the panelists that boards of directors are notorious for not doing succession planning. Not good. Irresponsible.

I updated my knowledge of the best practices for management succession by doing my due diligence and canvassing four Fortune 500 general counsels, two CEOs of different manufacturing companies, and three management consultants on their management succession plan templates. Although this was not a very scientific sampling, the polling gave me a sense of what companies were doing or not doing concerning planning for management succession.

Only one of the four Fortune 500 companies had a management succession plan. The other three and the non-Fortune 500 companies did not. Two management consultant companies did not have any templates or experience advising companies on succession plans and the third was working on developing one.

Of course everyone contacted thought it was a good idea to have a management succession plan, and some felt a little sheepish in admitting to not having a plan. A few of the ones who did not have a management succession plan said that there were occasional conversations at board meetings about resident executive "talent" that could be potential candidates for CEO succession.

Risk Management

We all have heard about major companies whose CEO became seriously ill or suddenly died. We also have heard where top layers of management have been decimated by catastrophic incidents like the 9/11 terrorist attacks on the World Trade Center Towers. Hurricane Katrina and the Japanese earthquake/tsunami nuclear power plant meltdown are additional reminders of how unanticipated disasters can wreak havoc on an unprepared company and its region.

Stockholders, investors, employees, and major customers certainly want to know what happens in "what if?" scenarios.

Mechanics of Making a Plan

In my updated research on management succession plans, I found three avenues that a company can take:

1. Do its own plan.

2. Buy software to do a plan.

3. Hire an outside consultant to help create a plan.

Basically, there are three degrees of planning:

1. Create a list of successors for important positions and make sure the successors have the leadership/management skills that are aligned with the mission, culture, and business strategy of the organization.

2. Develop an ongoing spreadsheet identifying, evaluating, and training/grooming executives and employees in multiple layers for many critical positions in the company.

3. Set up an elaborate system of back-up infrastructure and contingency plans for command and control in the event of emergencies.

Any one of the above degrees of planning requires a process that ultimately results in a document that a company can follow in the event of a succession.

Do What You Must Do

I suspect many executives and corporate boards feel about succession plans the way many individuals feel about estate planning: it is an unpleasant reminder of one's mortality that can be put off until tomorrow. No one likes to dwell on the time when one will not be around or will no longer be relevant.

I would wager that when Steve Jobs stepped down from Apple because of his illness, there was a succession plan in place to ensure a smooth transition.

Does your company have a succession plan? If not now, when? Initiate a plan.

Working through Crisis and Chaos

"Every great change is preceded by chaos."

~Deepak Chopra

Every executive or professional managing or leading people will face one or more periods of crises or chaos at her organization. It invariably will happen. Very few situations remain static indefinitely. What can you do when your organization undergoes stress or disruption that is damaging or fatal; or your organization has become ossified and is drifting toward unprofitability? Change it or watch it fade from existence — either quickly like Lehman Brothers or slowly and painfully like Sears. It does not have to happen and you do not have to preside over your company's demise even if it is in a dire or unstable condition.

I have had opportunities to discuss leadership values and insights with fellow alumni of the Leadership Greater Chicago Fellowship program, one of whom is **Ronald E. Daly**, a former president and CEO of Oce USA Holdings, former president of Donnelley Print Solutions, and a member of the corporate boards of directors of US Cellular and SuperValu. A few years ago Ron introduced me to the concept of initiating radical change to save or right an organization and referred to the "burning platform" change strategy that forward-looking business thought leaders have utilized.

Organizational change expert Daryl R. Connor developed the burning platform metaphor which comes from an oil rig worker having to decide to either stay on a burning oil rig and definitely die, or jump into the freezing, flaming-detritus-filled ocean and have a very high likelihood of dying. Either prospect carries a catastrophic risk, but the jump has the slight possibility of prolonged survival and maybe ultimate rescue.

This metaphor has been used to capsulize a leader's dilemma when facing the need for effecting radical change for the benefit of the business or organization. John P. Kotter, author of *Leading Change*, articulates a radical change model that Ron favors. Kotter's recommendation to create a sense of urgency concerning the necessity of change is akin to the burning platform impetus for radical change. Ron finds Kotter's approach compelling in that Kotter is forthright about the difficulty of achieving transformational change, but lays out a process for a rigorous change initiative. The obstacles will be fear, discomfort, and belief in the transiency of the latest corporate initiative. Ron goes on to say that the executive leader must show why the proposed changed state is superior to the status quo and why the current state of affairs cannot be sustainable.

I interviewed Ron, who had been the new president of Telecom Group at RR Donnelley, and he related to me his former company's case study on radical change.

Daly

I spent most of my career in the printing business at RR Donnelley. The year I became president of the Telecom Group, my group, like the rest of Donnelley, was faced with increasing competition, unstable commodity prices, rapidly changing technology, and customers aggressively seeking lower prices. I had an additional hurdle. Our board of directors had decided that Telecom was the most likely business to expand internationally. My boss let me know that I was expected to achieve this expansion without degrading profits from my U.S. business. To finance international growth, I had to find a way to make more profit.

From a cultural standpoint, Donnelley had a huge problem stemming from internal competition. For a very long time Donnelley had no external competition of our size and scale. The leaders of the business had set up internal competition between printing plants. The objective was to beat the other plants in efficiency so that your operation would be the best place for the sales force to bring sold work. This competition led to open hostility inside and a lack of attention to what outside competition was doing. Plants were very adept at using different accounting methods to measure throughput so comparisons were difficult. Sharing best practices was a no-no. This had to change.

Over the next five years we were able to implement a new business model. We moved away from the focus on being the low-cost provider. This original model had us lower costs so we could compete with lower prices. We moved to a model of customer intimacy. This model steered us toward being a solutions provider. In doing so, we had to learn so much about our customers that we probably knew more about them than they knew about themselves. In achieving this we became the industry thought leader. We used our knowledge, along with technology from other Donnelley printing markets, to bring new revenue-generating products to our customers. Becoming a part of our customers' revenue equation took pressure off the prices we were paid, as we got a premium over the competition.

On the cost side, we shed the idea that printing was a craft and not a science. Over the next five years we instituted statistical process control, multi-variable testing, six sigma, and 5S. We saw efficiency improve greatly and quality take huge leaps forward. We put in processes to stabilize our earnings. We developed a common dictionary and implemented activity-based costing that made comparisons and sharing easier.

We used quarterly business reviews, monthly conference calls, and yearly leadership conferences to work on the communications and cultural side of this change effort. We did lots of round tables to bring employees into the loop. We used a process called OGSM to cascade high-level objectives to the lowest levels of the organization, so that every employee knew their role in achieving our goal.

The market knowledge we had allowed us to become intimate with international publishers thirsty for ideas to grow their businesses. We were not a threat, unlike U.S. publishers trying to take market share from them. We helped them and we signed contracts to print for them. Being the low-price supplier wasn't what they wanted from us.

Over my seven years in Telecom, we became the most profitable of all the Donnelley printing businesses, we more than doubled the size of the business globally, we were the most efficient directory printer in the world, and we were the market leader on four continents. Kotter's model was instrumental in achieving this.

TAKE-AWAY:

Executive leadership is doing the tasks that others will not or cannot do.

CHAPTER NINE

PUTTING IT ALL TOGETHER

WHEN ALL IS SAID AND done, the theme and precepts in this book about executive success can be reduced to five basic principles that were best articulated by my late mother, Louise Antoinette Finch, an almost centenarian who reared six sons and a daughter to become achievers. Although we are far from perfect as individuals and have had our own share of ups and downs, and some of the siblings may be viewed as more materially successful than others, she obtained the same result from each of her children: all finished college and graduate or professional school. She fulfilled her life's purpose and left her legacy. How did she do that? She had a few maxims to live by that she drilled into us. These aphorisms would benefit anyone — executive, professional, and others — seeking to get a leg up in their career and in life.

1. My mother was big on standing up for yourself when another is perpetrating a wrong upon you or a family member or trying to diminish you or a family member. Mom taught us not to look for fights but not to allow ourselves to be victims. She led by example and did not wait around for my father to get home to go address an injustice at any level or push us out the door to face a bully. She made it clear that this attitude and posture must be based on our position being legitimate, ethical, and righteous, as well as our being without fault.

This maxim directly relates to understanding your rights, duties, obligations, opportunities, and benefits arising from any employment contract and separation agreement that you negotiate and any adverse office politics or personality differences or business disputes you may encounter.

2. When you start something, whether it is a project, a task, a job, an extracurricular activity, or a degree program, you must complete it. My mother abhorred quitters and lack of follow-through. She correctly knew that the lack of follow-through was a serious impediment to success. So despite unfair teachers, mean camp counselors, arbitrary coaches, or a tedious activity, we had to finish whatever program we started. To this day, my siblings and I talk about the little voice in our heads, when times got tough in medical, graduate, or law school, or in a demanding job, that repeated the mantra: "When you start something, you must finish it." At the time I made the decision to write a book, I knew that I must do it and to do otherwise was not an option.

   This maxim highlights the simple facts that you can never achieve anything without follow-through and that people will not want to work with you or do business with you if you are not reliable.

3. When we complained of being sick, whether severely or lightly, real or imagined, my mother would say, "Get up, wash your face, brush your teeth, put on your clothes, eat some breakfast, go to school, and, if you are still feeling lousy, then call me." By the time we did all those things,

our ailments seem to disappear or become sufficiently mitigated that we forgot that we were physically or psychologically under the weather. This was her way of saying:

a) have a strong work ethic;

b) show up to where you are supposed to be; and

c) adjust your attitude.

This anti-slacker and anti-lazy approach again carried me and my siblings through many a school and work day.

This maxim illustrates that bosses, colleagues, clients, and customers value those who go the extra mile to get the job done without complaint, no matter what the conditions or circumstances may be.

4. Surround yourself with quality people and people of integrity. Your friends and peers will make or break you, and you will be judged by the company you keep. I think of the hyper-academic high school, the Commonwealth School in Boston, that I was fortunate enough to be able to attend; the super-intellectual students there forced me to up my game and pull myself up from the mud of mediocrity. Counterintuitively, I did not find the competitive atmosphere intimidating because it actually inspired and stimulated me. My siblings and I have never gotten into serious trouble or arrested because our friends are sensible and have a lot of impulse control. A prison inmate laments about associating with the "wrong crowd" or blames a corrupting friend for his predicament. In short, choose your friends, associates, and peers very carefully.

This maxim embodies the saying that "Birds of a feather flock together" and the observation that high achievers surround themselves with other high achievers.

5. Don't lie or cheat. Being an honest person meant a lot to my mother. Character was the benchmark by which my mother evaluated people. She had an expression, "Pretty is as pretty does." A variant was, "Pretty on the inside is more important than being pretty on the outside."

This maxim emphasizes that trust and good character are critical in business and life. No one is going to entrust his or her affairs and business to a dishonest person.

Oftentimes you do not have to travel far to learn self-evident truths; they can be found within the four walls of your own upbringing without ever stepping outside your own front door.

I hear my mother's voice as I counsel my children about standing up to bullies, being honest, choosing their friends carefully, having a strong work ethic, and finishing what they start.

ACKNOWLEDGMENTS

I thank my wife, Carmen, and my children Marisol, Gabriella, and Maximelio, for providing me with the love and companionship that motivate me to strive and grow.

My brothers, Charles S. Finch III, M.D., Anthony P. Finch, Ph.D., and my niece, Aisha Finch, Ph.D. are my author role models. They preceded me in publishing books. It takes tenacity to write a book, and I admire those people who get it done.

My late mother, Louise Antoinette Finch, continues to be my inspiration to achieve things, and this book is the latest manifestation of her influence. I dedicate this book to her.

I am grateful for the opportunity to serve my executive and professional clients in advising them on their employment matters as they traverse their career paths. This book really is about, for, and as a result of them.

I truly appreciate the feedback from Fred H. Neu, an author and a friend, and from Jacqueline Moore, an editor and my cousin.

Lastly, a warm shout out to the team at Windy City Publishers for helping me to make this book happen.

NOTES

[1] Definition of felony: "The statutes or codes of several of the states define felony as any public offense or conviction of which the offender is liable to be sentenced to death or imprisonment in a penitentiary or state prison." (*Black's Law Dictionary*, Free Online Legal Dictionary 2nd Edition).

[2] Because this is a book that discusses both employment agreements and severance/separation agreements, which are contracts by another name, an executive can benefit from understanding some basic contract concepts.

One of these concepts is "consideration." A valid employment contract must comprise the elements of offer, acceptance, and consideration.

Consideration is a legal concept and is the bargained for exchange of promises or performances. "The test of a sufficient consideration is whether the act, forbearance or return promise results in a benefit to the promisor or a detriment to the promisee." (Laurence P. Simpson, *Contracts*, 2nd Edition, p. 80).

In an employment context, sufficient consideration to support an offer of employment would be the obligation to perform services by the employee and the obligation to pay wages/benefits/ and other compensation by the employer.

In a severance agreement, you may see a clause that reads something like this: "In consideration for signing this Agreement and complying with its terms, Employer agrees to pay Employee a total sum of $xxxx."

The Severance Agreement might state further that the parties agree that the contract clauses pertaining to severance payment and other compensation/benefits constitute sufficient consideration for this Agreement

Like all contracts, the terms of an employment agreement must also be clear and definite. Of course, we are not trying to turn our readers into lawyers, as we have too many as it is. Now when you hear a lawyer discussing contract issues and she says "there is a lack of consideration," you will now know she is not complaining about some rude, selfish person.

[3] See Endnote ii.

INDEX

ABOUT THE AUTHOR

G. A. FINCH

G. A. FINCH is a law firm partner in Chicago with over two decades of experience guiding executives, professionals and companies in their employment contracts and separation agreements. He has a blog, www.yourexecutivelife.com, which discusses employment contract and separation topics as well as non-legal matters like executive compensation, development, advancement, and leadership.

He attributes his ability to write reasonably well to his education at the Commonwealth School in Boston and at Amherst College. He is grateful for the opportunities of matriculating at the University of Michigan Law School and clerking for U.S. District Court Judge James B. Parsons. Those experiences empowered him to practice law with confidence and surefootedness.

He has been named an Illinois Super Lawyer, selected for the Leading Lawyers Network — The Top Lawyers, and designated the highest Martindale Hubbell Preeminent Rating in Legal Ability and Ethics. Salzburg Global Seminar and Leadership Greater Chicago, respectively, selected him to be one of their Fellows.

Finch has served on several non-profit, private, and governmental boards. He lives in the Sauganash neighborhood of Chicago with his wife, children, and cats.

Made in the USA
Lexington, KY
22 July 2019